NO
COMMON
GROUND

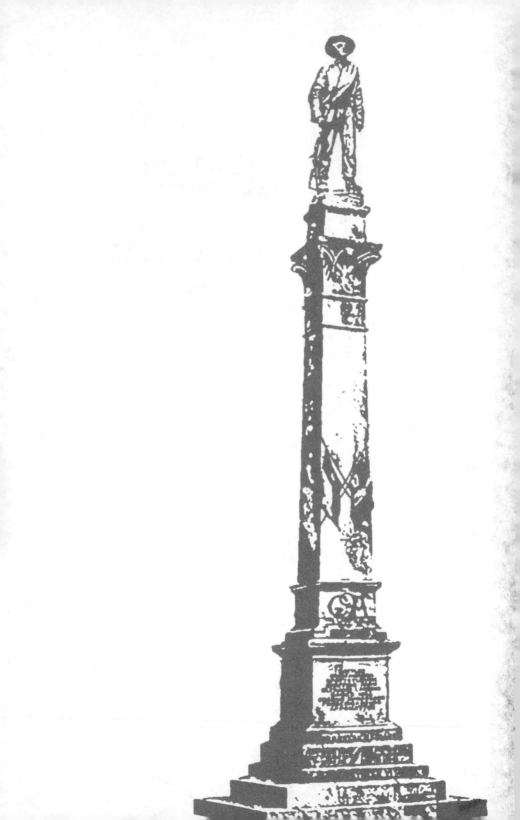

NO COMMON GROUND

Confederate Monuments and the
Ongoing Fight for Racial Justice

KAREN L. COX

A Ferris and Ferris Book

THE UNIVERSITY OF NORTH CAROLINA PRESS

Chapel Hill

Published under the

Marcie Cohen Ferris and William R. Ferris Imprint

of the University of North Carolina Press.

Set in Minion and DIN types

Manufactured in the United States of America

The University of North Carolina Press has been a member of the
Green Press Initiative since 2003.

Jacket illustration: demonstrators at the Robert E. Lee Monument
in Richmond, Va., on Wednesday, June 3, 2020. Photograph by
Jordan Vance.

Library of Congress Cataloging-in-Publication Data
Names: Cox, Karen L., 1962– author.
Title: No common ground: Confederate monuments and the
ongoing fight for racial justice / Karen L. Cox.
Description: Chapel Hill: The University of North Carolina Press,
[2021] | "A Ferris and Ferris book." |
Includes bibliographical references and index.
Identifiers: LCCN 2020051724 | ISBN 9781469662671 (cloth; alk.
paper) | ISBN 9781469662688 (ebook)
Subjects: LCSH: Soldiers' monuments—Social aspects—
Southern States—History. | Collective memory—Social aspects—
Southern States. | Protest movements—Southern States—
History. | Social movements—Southern States—History. |
White supremacy movements—Southern States—History. |
Racism—Southern States—History. | United States—History—
Civil War, 1861–1865—Monuments—Social aspects—
Southern States. | Confederate States of America—
Historiography. | Southern States—Race relations—History.
Classification: LCC E645 .C698 2021 | DDC 305.800975—dc23
LC record available at https://lccn.loc.gov/2020051724

For everyone
who speaks
truth to power

CONTENTS

FIGURES

NO COMMON GROUND

INTRODUCTION

Thirty-one years ago, I was working as a museum historian in Fayetteville, North Carolina, when I first encountered the United Daughters of the Confederacy (UDC), also commonly known as the Daughters. I was assisting a colleague and woodworker who had salvaged timber from the Confederate Women's Home that once stood in Fayetteville, and he wanted to know more about the home's origins. My research took me to the local library, where I culled through the microfilm of the local paper. The home, which opened in 1915, was the project of the UDC. Members had lobbied and received a $10,000 appropriation from the state legislature to construct the building and another $5,000 per year to maintain it.[1] This was an impressive amount of money at the time, but it was the dedication of the home that got my attention. The event took up the entire front page of the *Fayetteville Observer*. Political dignitaries from across the state, including a representative from the governor's office, attended the dedication.

What struck me was that during a time when women did not have the right to vote, *this* women's organization was clearly plugged in to the most powerful men in the state. It had gotten funds from the state legislature for its project, and these same men answered when the Daughters called them to be present for a dedication ceremony. I wanted to know more and began interviewing women who had been members of the organization ever since they had been drafted into the group's auxiliary, the Children of the Confederacy, and who knew the women behind the Confederate Women's Home. Over and over, I heard the words "powerhouse" in relation to these early UDC members, though I was only just beginning to grasp the impact of their work on the South.[2]

As I discovered in my research, the Daughters indeed made up the most powerful women's organization in the South in the early twentieth century. A group of 30 women founded the UDC in 1894 at a meeting in Nashville, Tennessee. Some of them had lived through the Civil War, while others had grown up in its aftermath. From this core group, the UDC grew rapidly into an organization of 100,000 by the First World War. Leaders established a wide-ranging agenda, but their fundamental mission was to shape the way future generations of white southerners remembered the Civil War, the Confederacy, and slavery, as well as to vindicate the men and women of the Confederate generation. Their efforts provided white southerners with a reason to take pride in Confederate heritage and to defend that heritage—including white supremacy—even in the face of a changing South.[3]

The enormous influence these southern women wielded provoked my curiosity and led me to write about their history and impact on southern culture in my first book, *Dixie's Daughters: The United Daughters of the Confederacy and the Preservation of Confederate Culture*. I dug into the history of, motivations for, and rituals surrounding Confederate monuments and the UDC's role in placing this statuary in cities and towns throughout the South and even outside of the region. At the time, I regarded the early twentieth century as a natural end point for my work, since the vast majority of the Daughters' statues were erected by World War I. I thought my work on this topic was complete.

But the history of Confederate monuments is not limited to those who built them or to those who venerated the Lost Cause. Rather, these monuments are part of a longer history that is also mired in racial inequality and modified by black resistance. And as events since 2015 have made clear, the monuments the Daughters built continue to maintain a tight hold on southern politics, southern history, and the southern landscape where they still stand.

Through a broad-based agenda to perpetuate Confederate memory, the Daughters gave inspiration to southern white men intent on dominating black southerners at every step, and by violence if necessary. Two generations removed from the Civil War, these women saw their efforts as part of an overall program of vindicating the Confederacy and those who sought to preserve it. Their battle to maintain Confederate culture—by perpetuating pro-southern history, educating white children, and yes, building monuments—required that the men of their generation be victorious in creating a southern power structure that their forefathers had failed to achieve. And they were. Those men established a political foundation based on white supremacy, disfranchised black men, compelled entire black communities into submission through racial violence, and wielded states' rights like a saber to thwart racial progress, while the federal government turned a blind eye and the Supreme Court upheld segregation.[4] While states' rights for the Confederate generation meant a state's right to maintain slavery, states' rights for the Jim Crow generation meant maintaining the racial status quo through laws and customs that gutted African Americans' rights as citizens, underfunded their schools, reenslaved them through mass incarceration, and made it nearly impossible for black southerners to break free from systems of inequality that limited where they could live and work.

African American efforts toward empowerment during Reconstruction did not fall by the wayside even during these reversals, nor did their explicit resistance against Confederate icons, including monuments. Generations later, it continues.

Confederate monuments are not innocuous symbols. Though in the past they were used by white southerners to teach about a mythological noble heritage completely stripped of the story of slavery, what they "teach" is not history. They are weapons in the larger arsenal of white supremacy, artifacts of Jim Crow not unlike the "whites only" signs that declared black southerners to be second-class citizens. Removing a monument from the public square is no more an act of erasing history than removing these signs from public accommodations. Just as history teaches us that those signs once existed, we can be assured that even after these monuments' removal, the books, photographs, postcards, unveiling speeches, old tourist brochures, and chamber of commerce promotional materials that documented them will continue to exist.

Removal, of course, does not mean certain destruction. Yes,

some statues have been damaged over the course of protests, but most have been removed to storage while cities determine their fate. Some have been moved to cemeteries for Confederate soldiers, and others await a calmer time when they might find a home on a battlefield park. Still others have been returned to the chapters of the UDC whose forebears first funded them. It could be that some Confederate monuments will be placed with museums of art or history where proper context can be provided, although some critics worry that such placement would mean creating shrines to the Confederacy.

The wide variety of possible fates for these monuments should come as no surprise, because most are intensely local objects.[5] How a city, town, or university determines the fate of its Confederate monument, or if it does nothing at all, will underscore that community's values, even when it doesn't reflect the wishes of the entire community. Yet once that decision is made and executed, it is important for these communities to grasp that the story is not over.

Removing a monument does not remove the systemic racism with which it has long been associated. It is a symbolic act only, although it may also serve as an important first step. The hard work of dismantling racism and honestly confronting racial inequality within that community must come next. After all, it was a movement against white supremacy that initially brought public concerns about Confederate monuments into the open. Today's protests against Confederate monuments, therefore, are but one stage in a much longer fight for racial justice.

■ ■ ■

Since 2015, Confederate monuments have transcended local debates to become a national issue. This is because such symbols challenge the narrative of American democracy and question whether there is truly "liberty and justice for all." Yet the escalation of this debate has led not to an honest conversation but to a polarization of political sides and a series of moves meant to further entrench Confederate monuments.

GOP legislators throughout the South have responded to the prospect of a reckoning on the local level through legislative schemes. In a number of southern states, monument laws, sometimes referred to as "heritage protection acts," have removed local communities' ability to make decisions about the future of the statues that dominate their town squares and courthouse lawns. These laws prevent local redress and make petitions meaningless. Often written by legislators who rose to positions of power through district gerrymandering, itself linked to voter suppression, these monument laws, in practice, invite continued protests and vandalism of monuments.

When these laws have proved insufficient to head off a growing movement, the federal government has inserted itself into the dispute. On June 26, 2020, President Donald J. Trump issued an executive order to further criminalize vandalism and "violence" against monuments across the United States, including Confederate statues in places where state and local authorities have removed them.[6] All the while, grassroots protests have persisted, and monuments have been vandalized and toppled as never before in American history, because citizens have been left with virtually no legal avenues for change.

Not all citizens are clamoring for monument removal. In November 2019, Elon University polled North Carolina residents on whether Confederate monuments should remain on public property. The poll's findings showed that a substantial majority of residents (65 percent) believed monuments should remain on government-owned property, although an even higher percentage favored adding contextual panels or plaques. According to political scientist James Husser, director of the Elon University poll, the difference of opinion essentially boiled down to differing perceptions of history. "Those viewing the Civil War as more about states' rights than slavery," Husser noted, were more likely to favor keeping monuments in place. The poll results also indicate how powerful the Lost Cause narrative remains.[7]

In an era defined by gerrymandering, voter suppression, and overwhelming displays of police violence, Confederate monuments have become a natural battleground for protests against systemic racism. The steady drumbeat of public outrage, legislative overreach, and local demonstrations reveals how the existing push and pull surrounding Confederate monuments has steadily escalated since the Charleston massacre in 2015.

In the aftermath of that tragedy, very few statues were removed, while new monument laws were passed and existing state laws were amended to make removal even more difficult. Following the violent white supremacy on display at the Unite the Right rally in Charlottesville in 2017, several more monuments were removed, some extralegally. Once more, states tightened their heritage laws and the push for removal again quieted, though only temporarily.

The police killing of George Floyd, a forty-six-year-old black man, on May 25, 2020, in Minneapolis reignited the struggle. White police officers arrested Floyd for allegedly paying for cigarettes with a counterfeit twenty-dollar bill, then wrestled him to the ground. After Floyd's hands were tied behind his back, Officer Derek Chauvin placed his knee on Floyd's neck and held it there for eight minutes and forty-six seconds, cutting off his ability to breathe and causing his death.[8] George Floyd's murder, which was videotaped by bystanders, set off a series of massive Black Lives Matter protests across the United States and around the globe. And in the South, those protests took aim at Confederate statues, most notably on Richmond, Virginia's Monument Avenue.

Many monuments were covered in graffiti and some were ripped from their pedestals, because what protesters saw in George Floyd's death was what they saw symbolized by Confederate monuments—white supremacy and systemic racism. The intensity of these protests presented numerous southern cities and towns with a crisis. Many hoped to avoid a scenario similar to that in Richmond but were hamstrung by their own state's draconian monument laws as well as by the very real fear of white supremacist backlash and violence. Nonetheless, several statues were removed, either in spite of those laws or because local governments used loopholes to facilitate their removal.

Monument removals during the summer of 2020 led journalists and scholars alike to wonder aloud whether this represented a turning point in the history of Confederate monuments. Significantly more statues were being removed than after events in Charleston or Charlottesville. Was this the end of their dominion over the southern landscape?

In reality, the total number of removals represented a small percentage of Confederate monuments overall. The Southern

Poverty Law Center (SPLC) has documented more than 1,700 monuments, markers, and memorials that have been dedicated to the Confederacy over the course of U.S. history. Of this number, approximately 750 to 800 are Confederate statues. Popular rhetoric about the demise of Confederate monuments in the South has been greatly exaggerated, to say the least.

Even the number of monuments that currently stand is difficult to pin down with certainty. The SPLC data set on Confederate symbols is an ongoing project, so the numbers that appear in media accounts, including several news items based on data mining, fluctuate somewhere between 771 and 830 monuments. As recently as the spring of 2020, however, some news outlets erroneously presented the 1,700 figure as the total number of monuments (rather than the total of monuments and other markers and memorials).[9] Given the wide variance, I traveled to Montgomery, Alabama, in early March 2020, just before the COVID-19 quarantine, where I met with members of the SPLC team responsible for the report on monuments published under the title "Whose Heritage?," which is based on the organization's data collection.[10] When I asked what they made of the discrepancy in figures in the press, the response was, "We created the data set. We cannot control how it gets used." Ultimately, allowing for important caveats related to the precision of these numbers, I believe that the figure of 750 to 800 monuments represents a fair estimate of those erected. Even allowing for the most recent wave of monument removals, several hundred remain.

The difficulty in making sense of how many statues are out there is indicative of just how much remains unsettled about the timeline of monument building over the past century. We know that the vast majority were erected in the period between 1890 and 1920. Yet another narrative that emerged in the media since the SPLC data were released is that a second "explosion" of monument building occurred during the civil rights era.[11] This may have to do with a report issued by the Equal Justice Initiative claiming that there were "scores of new monuments" built at midcentury.[12] While in Montgomery, I also met with an Equal Justice Initiative attorney who, unlike the SPLC team, would not provide the organization's data. The SPLC data do not confirm a significant increase in monument building at midcentury — and until the Equal Justice Initiative can show its work, historians, journalists, and those studying this history should rely on the SPLC's data. This means that while there *were* new monuments built in the 1950s and 1960s, the most reliable numbers reveal that approximately only twenty statues were erected in each decade, some of which were part of the Civil War centennial celebration that was taking place at the height of the civil rights movement, between 1961 and 1965.[13] And while the final tally of how many hundreds of Confederate monuments were built over the last 150 years may hint at the considerable funds and efforts put toward their construction, this raw number does not provide us with a full accounting of the history of Confederate monuments.

This book offers a place to start. As its chapters reveal, the real story of Confederate monuments is about how existing monuments became flashpoints in the crusade for white supremacy, as well as in the struggle for civil rights. To understand their history is to understand how white southerners memorialized men who fought in a war to preserve slavery and created a "new" South that sought to limit the freedom of black southerners whose ancestors were enslaved. Yet at the same time, to *fully* understand their history is also to understand how generations of black southerners have demonstrated their scorn for monuments they have always believed were symbols of slavery and oppression. This places Confederate statues, especially those that sit on the grounds of courthouses and state capitols, at the center of the ongoing fight for racial justice.

What does it mean to say that there is "no common ground" where Confederate monuments are concerned? Generations of white southerners have shared the belief that these symbols represented a particular "southern heritage" imbued with nostalgia for Confederate soldiers that also erases slavery as a cause of war. Conversely, generations of black southerners have regarded Confederate monuments as honoring men who fought to perpetuate human slavery. These competing interpretations began soon after the Civil War ended and have remained intact ever since. Neither side has budged, and there has been no common ground about what these monuments mean — not even in the physical spaces where they stand. What should have been common ground—democratic spaces where votes were cast, justice was decided, local laws were passed, and ordinary people lived out their lives—has been dominated by statues whose very existence condemned black southerners to second-class citizenship. Where such symbols continue to stand unchallenged, what common ground can be found?

■ ■ ■

Three decades after beginning my research into the UDC, it seemed as though I couldn't escape the history of Confederate monuments, no matter how much I wanted to put it behind me. By the fall of 2019, I had spent two years giving talks about Confederate monuments at universities, museums, libraries, and for community groups. I was sick of talking about the damned monuments; returning to the Lost Cause and the people who distorted southern history and propped up white supremacy for a century and a half after losing the Civil War was the last thing I wanted to do.

Community organizers helped to change my mind. In February 2018, a group committed to improving the city of Louisville, Kentucky, for all citizens invited me to participate in the West Louisville Forum, which inspired me.[14] That talk and another I gave in Morganton, North Carolina, in January 2020 were both organized by ministers, one African American and one white. Interracial groups of more than 200 people attended each event, revealing that ordinary people hungered for a better understanding of the role Confederate monuments have played in their communities.

I was also inspired by the story of a thirty-nine-year-old woman named LaPeachra Bell from Shreveport, Louisiana. I discovered her through a 2018 documentary produced by the *New York Times* called "Taking a Knee and Taking Down a Monument." Bell's son, who played for his high school football team, wanted to take a knee as a display of solidarity with former NFL quarterback Colin Kaepernick. Bell realized that if her son could take a stand for something he believed in, she could too. So, she spoke before the Shreveport City Council about removing the Confederate monument that had stood on the Caddo Parish Courthouse grounds since 1905.

Their convictions came with consequences for the Bell family, who faced vicious racial hatred in response to their stance against racism, but they stayed strong. I reached out to offer Ms. Bell moral support, because I understood the stakes as much as she did. She told me that she had "received some disturbing messages." In a later exchange, I wrote that from her example I learned what real courage looks like. She brushed me off and in the process told me something that has stuck with me ever since. "Please don't give me credit for this," she replied; "It was done because I'm desperate. I just wanted to make sure my children [have] a better world and not have to repeat history."[15] Women like LaPeachra Bell should never be desperate to be heard or taken seriously.

■ ■ ■

This book tells the history of Confederate monuments since 1865 through the debates that surrounded them and the movements that arose to erect, defend, oppose, and remove them. It is focused on community-based monuments rather than those erected on battlefields because it is in communities where debates over the meaning of these statues have primarily taken place. The story begins with the Lost Cause, how white southerners came to enshrine that idea in stone, and how their reshaping of the southern landscape shored up a revisionist narrative of the Civil War. At the same time, the book documents an African American legacy of protest against Confederate statues that surfaced as the first ones were being erected in the nineteenth century. In the chapters that follow, Confederate monuments are revealed to sit at the intersection of so much that shaped the South in the twentieth and twenty-first centuries, including Jim Crow segregation, racial violence, civil rights marches, southern politics, the rise of neo-Confederates, and grassroots activism.

Every one of the hundreds of Confederate monuments that dot the southern landscape has a history, as do those that have been removed. More often than not they are local histories that include women in the UDC, white male power brokers, the black laborers who helped build the foundations on which monuments were placed, unveiling rituals, Confederate Memorial Day ceremonies, racial violence, and social protest. This book does not seek to provide a comprehensive history of each and every statue that exists; rather, it places the subject of Confederate monuments in its proper historical context and explores how these objects have been used by a variety of historical actors whose motivations also varied.

There are many ways in which a book on the history of Confederate monuments can be written. I fully expect other historians will add to this literature. I also believe that scholars representing different disciplines, from art historians to sociologists to political scientists, can expand our discussions about Confederate monuments, as many already have.[16] This is my contribution. It is the product of thirty-plus years of wrangling with these statues and the women who placed them there. The stark new light that recent events have cast on these statues reveals how their long dominion over the southern landscape has affected the history of the South, the nation, and all Americans. But how to reckon with that history is up to the communities living in the monuments' shadows.

1

REWRITING
HISTORY
IN STONE

In order to understand monuments of any kind, it is important to grasp the intentions and motivations of those who sought to erect a monument in the first place. This holds true for Confederate monuments, which have dominated the southern landscape for more than 150 years. They were placed there by white southerners whose intentions were not to preserve history but to glorify a heritage that did not resemble historical facts. By erecting these statues, white southerners have, over time, upheld a past in which the ideals of Confederate nationalism rest on metaphorical pedestals of heroism and sacrifice, while at the same time they negate the legacy of slavery and suggest that all white southerners were committed to the Confederate cause, which they were not.[1]

Over time, monument supporters concocted new language to defend the South's monuments or to employ them in the defense of the region itself. In the 1950s, the Confederate tradition expanded to include Cold War rhetoric that warned southern whites that the civil rights movement and federal intrusion were linked to communism. In the immediate post–civil rights era, words like "equality" were employed in the defense of monuments, while during the era of multiculturalism, supporters argued the need to protect "Confederate American" heritage. During the post-9/11 years, monument defenders likened removal to the Taliban's destruction of cultural artifacts. The target kept shifting because the statues were not about history; rather, they symbolized something even more precious to the cause of white supremacy—protecting the southern way of life.

Consequently, it is not a stretch to argue that removing a monument is not removing history, at least not the history of the Confederacy. Rather, the real history of these statues and markers is about their impact as objects of reverence for many white southerners, though not all, and as painful reminders of slavery and Jim Crow for generations of black southerners. And, as historian Malinda Maynor Lowery has written, the history of Confederate monuments "also erase[s] Indians—as well as Asians, Middle Easterners, Latinos, and other diverse peoples who call the South home."[2] Understanding the fundamentals of that history is essential if communities are to make informed decisions about what to do with the statues in their midst. The ultimate purpose of the pages that follow is to provide the historical foundation that will allow readers to grasp where these monuments fit in the history of the post–Civil War South and all that came after.

To begin, monuments are not just pillars of stone without meaning; every monument also represents a system of beliefs. Nor are they purely static objects; the groups who erected them, whether ladies' memorial associations, the United Daughters of the Confederacy, or the men's organizations that have built the most recent ones, did not just put them up and walk away. Throughout their history, Confederate monuments became reanimated on an annual basis through rituals held on Confederate Memorial Day and on the birthdays of Confederate generals, during Civil War reenactments, and in the protests against their removal. There is also a distinction to be made between memorials and monuments. While memorials serve to commemorate the dead through a special day or in a public space, they are not monuments. On the other hand, monuments are always a type of memorial. For more than a century, white southerners have gathered around these memorials to recall the Confederate past and reassert their commitment to the values of their ancestors, the very same values that resulted in a war to defend slavery and expand the institution. Thus, whether they stand on courthouse lawns or in cemeteries, and regardless of the additional meanings they have taken on over the course of 150 years of history, Confederate statues have always been attached to the cause of slavery and white supremacy.

The connection between white supremacy and Confederate monuments is not an exaggeration or an after-the-fact revisionist interpretation. Confederate veterans openly used the term "Anglo-Saxon supremacy," which today we simply refer to as white supremacy. It appeared repeatedly in unveiling speeches as a badge of honor for the men who helped reverse the gains made by freedmen during Reconstruction. The Ku Klux Klan and its first grand wizard, Confederate general Nathan Bedford Forrest, were applauded for restoring racial order to the South through tactics of violence and intimidation against African Americans. In 1914 Laura Martin Rose, a UDC member from Mississippi, published a booklet on the KKK that was endorsed by both the UDC and the Sons of Confederate Veterans as a publication that should be placed in school libraries. She hoped that it would "inspire" white southern youth "with respect and admiration for the Confederate soldiers," who, she wrote, "were the real Ku Klux." These "sturdy white men of the South," she declared, "maintained white supremacy and secured Caucasian civilization," later adding that during Reconstruction their efforts helped "to maintain the supremacy of the white race."[3]

Southern whites after the Civil War were overwhelmingly preoccupied with coming up with a narrative to explain their defeat. Any book about Confederate culture and its evolution following the Civil War, therefore, must begin with understanding how white southerners came to terms with that defeat, how they justified their failure to create a separate nation, and how they outright rejected the idea that slavery was a primary cause of the Civil War. To do so requires an examination of the evolving postwar narratives about the Old South, the Confederacy, and even Reconstruction — all of which revolve around what Confederates and their descendants called the "Lost Cause."

White southerners were first aided in their efforts to explain not only what went wrong but also why their cause was just by Edward A. Pollard, the wartime journalist for the *Richmond Examiner*. In 1866 Pollard, a native Virginian, wrote a tome he titled *The Lost Cause: A New Southern History of the War of the Confederates*. A "new" southern history immediately suggested that this was intended as a partisan assessment of the war even as the first histories of the war were just being published. Over the course of 752 pages, Pollard laid out a Confederate account of the war as well as a narrative that proved useful to white southerners reeling from defeat and the devastation of their world. Not only did he coin the term "Lost Cause," but he provided former Confederates with a rhetorical balm to soothe their psychological wounds. In doing so, he helped lay the foundation of a mythology that reassured them that their cause was just and their values worth fighting for even in the face of a thoroughly crushing defeat.[4]

Born into the planter class of Nelson County, Virginia, in 1832, Pollard grew up on a wealthy plantation worked by more than 100 slaves and was an ardent defender of the South's "peculiar institution." In 1859, when he was a young man of twenty-eight, he earned fame from the publication of *Black Diamonds Gathered in the Darkey Homes of the South*, a book in the form of a series of letters with David Clark, an attorney from Newburgh, New York, wherein Pollard offered a robust defense of slavery. Alongside romanticized portraits of the enslaved he personally knew growing up on his father's plantation, Pollard's letters rationalized keeping human beings enslaved while also offering a pointed critique of abolitionist writers like Harriet Beecher Stowe, author of *Uncle Tom's Cabin*, whom he disparagingly referred to as "n****r worshippers."[5]

Pollard wrote about the South from a position of class privilege. He grew up as a member of the slave-owning planter class and, because of the increasing pressure placed on that group by northern abolitionists, offered what became the standard defense of slavery then and, in some circles, even today. In effect, he argued for slavery's "civilizing" influence. Writing to Clark from Virginia in 1858, he asserted, "The American institution of slavery does not depress the African but elevates him in the scale of social and religious human being." Two pages later he repeats himself:

"I think the remarkable characteristic of our *'peculiar institution'* in improving the African race humanly, socially, and religiously, is alone sufficient to *justify* it." Pollard's use of the term "African" and "African race" was commonplace. It mattered not that for more than a century the expansion of slavery had resulted from natural increase, nor that the enslaved were no longer "African" in the truest sense of the word. By this time they were as Virginian as Pollard.[6]

Pollard's ideas about slavery were in keeping with this vociferous defense of southern nationalism. Like other men of his class, he believed in the superiority of southern culture, economic self-sufficiency based on plantation slavery, and the desire for regional independence. The North's form of capitalism, he argued, debased workers in the form of "wage slavery" and neglected their basic needs, unlike those slaves in the South who were fed, clothed, and cared for in their old age. The South, therefore, was the antithesis of what Pollard called the "garish" North. Further, white southerners were the true caretakers of the nation's constitutional heritage. In effect, by every measure, the South was superior to the North.

The Confederate generation's undying faith in southern nationalism and belief that southern culture was superior to that of the North made defeat a hard pill to swallow. *The Lost Cause* became Pollard's paean to southern nationalism and a rally cry to not give up on it. The war might be over, but the fight to maintain the region's values still existed. The fight for Confederate independence, according to Pollard and those who followed in his footsteps, was reinvented in order to align with the South's postwar reality.

As a Lost Cause evangelist, Pollard gave future generations the language and arguments to defend white supremacy and dismiss slavery as a cause of war. That those of the Confederate generation were the rightful heirs of the Revolutionary generation was just one argument that played out repeatedly for decades, particularly the South's defense of the Tenth Amendment to the Constitution, which preserves states' rights. A second argument, a complete reinterpretation of southern nationalism, was that slavery had been necessary to preserve the racial status quo and prevent race war. Pollard and others still justified slavery as a paternalistic system that benefited the enslaved, but in the shadow of defeat, it now needed to be seen as necessary. This narrative allowed Confederate soldiers to be understood as defenders not of slavery but of the region and their race. In sum, these false memories of the Confederacy still had value, even in defeat. The Lost Cause, therefore, was nothing to lament. It was a "just cause," and in the postwar South, white supremacy was front and center.[7]

Pollard stood firm in his conviction of the justness of the South's cause. In the conclusion to his book on the war, he remained convinced of the superiority of Confederate soldiers and suggested that the war had proved nothing. "The Confederates have gone out of this war," he wrote, "with the proud, secret, *dangerous* consciousness that they are THE BETTER MEN, and that there was nothing wanting but a change in a set of circumstances and a firmer resolve to make them victors." That lack of resolve, for Pollard, fell directly on the shoulders of Jefferson Davis and his administration, not on the larger populace of the South.[8] In effect, white southerners did not lose the war; their leaders failed them.

Pollard also argued that despite the war's outcome, the South did not have to admit to defeat but rather only to what was "properly decided." For him, only two issues were determined in 1865—the restoration of the Union and a legal end to slavery. "It did not decide negro equality; it did not decide negro suffrage; it did not decide State Rights . . . and these things which the war did not decide, the southern people still cling to," he proclaimed. In this, Pollard was prophetic. White southerners absolutely held fast to the supremacy of their race and used it as a means to control the formerly enslaved, even in the face of Reconstruction.[9]

Reconstruction, the twelve-year period that followed the Civil War when it ended in 1865, sought to reunify the nation but also assist newly emancipated men and women with the transition from slavery to citizenship. It required the existence of federal troops and officials in the states of the former Confederacy to ensure that former Confederates complied with the changes to laws, including constitutional amendments that abolished slavery, made freedmen citizens, and gave black men the right to vote. Reconstruction also resulted in the creation of the Freedmen's Bureau, run by federal officials, to support African Americans as they adapted to their freed status. For white southerners, who called Reconstruction the "Tragic Era," these changes were an insult added to the injury of defeat and destruction throughout large swaths of the region.

Even before Pollard published *The Lost Cause,* southern states instituted "black codes" to control the movement of freed people, using older "vagrancy" laws to arrest and punish black men and women for being "idle" and forcing black children into "apprenticeships" with their former masters. Colonel Samuel Thomas, a Freedmen's Bureau official assigned to Vicksburg, Mississippi, testified before Congress in 1865 that former Confederates "are yet unable to conceive of the Negro as possessing any rights at all." As he further explained, "The whites esteem the blacks their property by natural right, and however much they may admit that the individual relations of masters and slaves have been destroyed by the war and the President's emancipation proclamation, they still have an ingrained feeling that the blacks at large belong to the whites at large, and whenever opportunity serves they treat the colored people just as their profit, caprice or passion may dictate."[10] Reconstruction took on an added urgency because of testimony like Thomas's, and Congress took action by ratifying the Fourteenth Amendment in 1868, providing freedmen with citizenship, and the Fifteenth Amendment in 1870, which provided for black male suffrage—the very rights that Pollard claimed the war had not decided.

White southerners never fully accepted former slaves as citizens, and once federal troops had completely withdrawn from the region in 1877, southern state legislatures immediately sought ways to reverse the rights Reconstruction had given them. Those efforts were ramped up in 1890 when Mississippi, led by one of its U.S. senators, James Z. George, ratified a new state constitution whose primary purpose was to disfranchise black male voters, reversing the rights afforded them by the Fifteenth Amendment. Known as the "Mississippi Plan," it added a poll tax of two dollars to vote and what became popularly known as the "understanding clause" that required voters to be able to read any section of the state constitution or "be able to understand the same when read to him or give a reasonable interpretation thereof." While these changes also affected poor whites, their primary target was black voters. Throughout the 1890s, other southern legislatures followed suit and changed their state constitutions to include a poll tax and an understanding clause.

By 1901, black men had effectively been disfranchised in all the states of the former Confederacy. Alongside these legal machinations, southern lawmakers were assisted in their efforts by vigilante groups like the Ku Klux Klan and other white men who used violence to intimidate black men and prevent them from voting. Together, they reclaimed the region under the hood of white supremacy, reversing the effects of the Reconstruction amendments intended to provide blacks meaningful citizenship.

These were the political and racial realities of the South as Confederate monuments were being built. White men enacted Jim Crow laws from their state legislatures, while in the streets they practiced "lynch law"—extralegal racial violence to bring African Americans into compliance. Eliminating black men from political office and reasserting control of the public square also had an unintended effect—it cleared the way for white women to assume a public role in the campaign of white supremacy through monument building.

■ ■ ■

The earliest monuments were built in cemeteries as a means of honoring the Confederate dead who were buried there. That effort was begun by women who formed ladies' memorial associations after the war. Their work continued and expanded after Reconstruction as statues started to appear outside of cemeteries and, in the 1890s, began to reshape the public landscape. The most famous example of this change was in Richmond, Virginia, where an enormous equestrian statue of Robert E. Lee was unveiled in May 1890. Lesser known monuments were also built throughout the South in parks and along boulevards and main streets.

The most common site for building Confederate monuments was on the grounds of local courthouses and state capitols, which today makes them the most controversial of all Confederate memorials. Often placed directly in front of the courthouse, these monuments have claimed the public square for southern whites, spaces that for more than a century have been not simply white-controlled but also shaped by segregation. Inside the courthouse or statehouse, white men made laws that served as a cudgel against African American equality, while outside, the Lost Cause narrative became ritualized through annual observations of Confederate Memorial Day.

Confederate commemorative activity helped reinforce another form of white supremacist messaging at courthouses and state-houses—racial violence. As Sherrilyn Ifill writes in her book, *On the Courthouse Lawn*, courthouses were "a deliberate choice of venue for lynchings." While Ifill's book is focused on the Eastern Shore of Maryland, her claim carries weight in other parts of the South where public spaces were "used to enforce the message of white supremacy, often violently." Lynch mobs often overpowered local sheriffs, some of whom were complicit, removing black prisoners located in the jails adjacent to courthouses only to lynch them in front of the courthouse itself. As Ifill points out, these and other lynchings were not community secrets. Members of the local white community knew about them and were often complicit in these violent acts, which were frequently committed in public. Hundreds and sometimes thousands attended these spectacles.[11]

Those who argue that Confederate monuments are simply about heritage willfully ignore the historical and physical contexts in which they were built. It is nearly impossible to ascribe innocent veneration of the war dead to those who constructed Confederate monuments, especially during the rise of Jim Crow and racial violence. Building a monument to the Confederacy on grounds where laws were made or upheld, especially during the heyday of the UDC between the mid-1890s and World War I, symbolized more than paying homage to Confederate heroes. Courthouse lawns are supposed to be democratic public spaces, since they surround the building where citizens engage with their government. Given that, it is important to understand that statues were placed adjacent to courthouses with the full support of local white men—attorneys, judges, and sheriffs—who worked inside their walls. Therefore, a Confederate monument, especially one that rose several feet in the air so that it could not go unnoticed or was stationed directly in front of courthouse doors, was an intentional statement about who made laws and who enforced them.

And in the Jim Crow period, those laws very often sought to do one of two things: keep African Americans as second-class citizens or incarcerate them.

The practical uses of these monuments, especially those alongside courthouses, both reveal and reinforce their true meaning. These statues have often been the site of gatherings during moments of racial unrest, precisely because they stand on government landscapes in the center of towns, counties, or parishes. The truth is that the same white citizens who gathered to watch a black man get lynched in their town were often the same white citizens who gathered for the unveiling of a Confederate monument. A community complicit in racial violence was often the same community that raised a monument honoring the Confederacy and the values it represented, several decades removed from secession.

Those values are historically tied to slavery, and still monument defenders continue to argue that Confederates went to war to defend states' rights, leaving out the fact that states' rights meant the right to perpetuate slavery. This is a fact that Confederate vice president Alexander Stephens made clear in his famous "Cornerstone Speech" in 1861, only a few weeks before the Civil War erupted. Not only was the Confederacy founded on the notion that "the negro is not equal to the white man," Stephens argued, but "slavery subordination to the superior race is his natural and normal condition." *This is white supremacy.* The ardent southern nationalist Edward Pollard, writing in the immediate aftermath of Confederate defeat, also maintained that a central aim of the cause was to maintain white rule. Their statements, and those of hundreds of their contemporaries, demonstrate that one cannot separate Confederate monuments from the culture of white supremacy that the Confederacy itself represented.[12]

■ ■ ■

Confederate monuments have been—and still are—used for purposes other than honoring ancestors or southern "heritage." Education was central to the builders' goals. By the time the UDC had taken the lead in monument building in the early twentieth century, the statues had become instructional tools for schoolchildren. The Daughters, some of whom were public schoolteachers, recognized monuments' import for informing children about the past, so they involved children in the annual rituals of Confederate Memorial Day or took students to their local monument for history lessons, reinforcing the classroom lessons of Confederate heroes and the Lost Cause. These kinds of rituals continued until public schools were desegregated, which in some districts did not occur until the 1970s. One UDC member I interviewed in the early 1990s told me that when schools were desegregated, Confederate Memorial Day—a day that ended up with ceremonies around the Confederate monument in Fayetteville, North Carolina—"just wasn't the same." When I asked her why, she remarked that it was because there were now black students in what had previously been the all-white high school marching band that participated in these ceremonies. Her response provided insight into the intimate connections between monuments, white public schools, and town celebrations of the Confederate past—and recognized the threat that even the slightest gesture toward racial equality posed to the status quo.

If we are to understand Confederate monuments and their meaning, we must examine the various cultural and political contexts within which they were built. These memorials have generally been erected as a response to vexing times, and for many white southerners, those times have reflected changes in race relations. The boom period of monument building began in the 1890s, which accompanied not only the rise of the UDC but also an expansion of racial violence in response to black progress in the South. Many southern women were on board with such a response, especially Georgian Rebecca Latimer Felton. Like many white southerners of her day, she subscribed to the belief that black men were the greatest threat to rural white women and that lynching was the best deterrent. Speaking in 1897 to members of the Georgia Agricultural Society, she said, "If it needs lynching to protect women's dearest possession from ravening beasts, then I say lynch, a thousand times a week if necessary."[13]

During the peak period of monument building, members of the Confederate generation—veterans and their wives—were dying off. This further spurred the UDC to action. Members sought to demonstrate devotion to their Confederate forebears and did so as part of a broader agenda to shape the culture of the South, which was focused not only on the past but on the future. The Daughters always believed, and it is stated directly in their constitution, that each action they took was to perpetuate the values of the Confederate generation "unto the third and fourth generations." In other words, Confederate culture was meant to continue and be carried forth by future generations of white southerners. Monuments were very much a part of that vision.

The construction of monuments didn't come to a stop after the First World War. In fact, they have been erected in every decade since the Civil War. Another small uptick in monument building occurred in the South during the mid-twentieth century, as between thirty and forty monuments were raised between 1950 and 1969.[14] Certainly, the Civil War centennial celebrations from 1961 to 1965 figured into the creation of new statues and memorials. At the same time, monuments were front and center as the civil rights movement gained momentum. The role of these statues at midcentury, therefore, was about a clash of values in the South — those that were forward-looking and guided by the goals of racial equality versus those still shaped by the fabricated narratives of the Lost Cause and a commitment to segregation and white supremacy.

The most recent surge in monument building has occurred since 2000. In this case, the South has witnessed the erection of thirty-five new monuments, several generations removed from the Civil War. The group responsible for this latest spate has been the Sons of Confederate Veterans (also known as the SCV or the Sons). The Civil War sesquicentennial took place between 2011 and 2015, yet other societal changes have been in play as well. White anxiety about racial progress served as the backdrop to earlier periods of monument expansion, and the same has been true since 2000.

Several reasons have figured into the continued memorialization of the Confederacy over the last two decades. First, in a complete reversal from the history of a century ago, UDC members have ceded this responsibility to their white male counterparts in the SCV. The Sons' numbers have grown, and many may also hold membership in the League of the South, formed in 1994. The League of the South is an explicitly racist group dedicated to the creation of an "Anglo-Celtic" Christian state that would politically dominate black people and other minorities, and it often employs Confederate iconography. Second, there has been a steady rise in anti-immigrant sentiment since 9/11, as well as a backlash to the perceived racial progress of electing the United States' first black president, Barack Obama. Third, over the last decade, hate groups with ties to white nationalism have rapidly expanded, many of which welcomed the presidency of Donald Trump. In fact, Richard B. Spencer, the white nationalist leader who helped organize the Charlottesville Unite the Right rally in 2017, claimed that "there is no question that [the rally in] Charlottesville wouldn't have happened without Trump."[15] To be clear, this book does not argue that there is a direct cause-and-effect relationship between these developments and monument building. However, the defense of Confederate monuments that was visible in the rally in Charlottesville, combined with the nostalgia attached to white southern heritage that is a central tenet of the Lost Cause, fits well within the realm of white nationalist beliefs.

Just as we need to grasp the history behind the reasons white southerners built monuments, we must also understand the long-standing tradition that countered this kind of memorialization. African Americans have participated in a tradition of protest against Confederate monuments and the Lost Cause since the late nineteenth century. Black communities throughout the South have used their counter-memories of slavery, Reconstruction, and Jim Crow to combat the one-sided narratives that these statues represent. There is also a long history of public critiques of Confederate monuments. Certainly, national black leaders like Frederick Douglass and W. E. B. Du Bois criticized them, but in this they were not alone, as some of the most vociferous opponents were black southerners for whom a Confederate statue in their community represented a personal attack on their citizenship and, indeed, their lives. Yet it is also true that opposition was not universal among black southerners any more than support for Confederate monuments was universal among white southerners.

The bottom line is that Confederate monuments cannot be boiled down to the Lost Cause catchphrase "They're about southern heritage." The chapters that follow seek to complicate what we think we know about Confederate monuments and to clarify what makes them controversial, especially in the twenty-first century. Though aggressive critiques of their presence on the southern landscape emerged in the aftermath of Charlottesville, this book attempts to document the much longer history of African Americans contesting these symbols through both word and deed.

National conversations, statewide opinion polls on removing monuments, or the presence, real or imagined, of out-of-town protesters and counterprotesters might inflame debates, but none of these solves what is, essentially, a local problem. In speaking to communities on this subject, I'm often asked, "What should we do about this?" My reply is always the same: "This is a community decision." Any decisions made must include representation from a cross-section of community stakeholders. It requires goodwill and cannot take place in secret.

There are hundreds of Confederate monuments that still cast their shadow over the American South, and many communities will not achieve the goal of having honest discussions about what to do with their monument. But if they do, they will need to ask themselves, "Does a monument honoring the Confederacy represent our community's values in the twenty-first century?"

Confederate statues were built alongside the history of Lost Cause myth and fabrication and in a culture of white supremacy and violence. They are not simply honorific objects made of stone, bronze, or marble. They reflect back to society the beliefs with which they are imbued, whether placed there by a ladies' memorial association in 1865 or the Sons of Confederate Veterans in 2019. What follows begins with those memorial associations and tracks the longer history of the Lost Cause to show how monuments mirror the values of the generation who built them and the later generations who defended them, as well as the legacy of African American protest of these statues in the ongoing fight for racial justice since the Civil War.

2

FROM
BEREAVEMENT
TO
VINDICATION

In January 1867, the Hollywood Memorial Association, a group of white women organized after the Civil War for the purpose of caring for the graves in Richmond's Hollywood Cemetery, invited George Wythe Munford to deliver a lecture. Munford, born in the city in 1803, had been an active civil servant before the Civil War, holding the office of secretary of the Commonwealth of Virginia for twelve years until 1864, and was once considered a serious candidate for governor. But in the aftermath of Confederate defeat and in the face of federal occupation of the city, the sixty-four-year-old Munford felt like a man without a country.

At the time of his lecture in 1867, Munford was still angry. He began by inviting his audience to join him in that anger by reminding them of how, in 1864, federal forces burned down the Virginia Military Institute and pillaged nearby Washington College. "If aliens to our soil can mutilate and deface the college . . . demolish its apparatus, and destroy its libraries," he fumed, "what may they not do?" As far as he was concerned, federal authorities had denied white southerners their constitutional liberty: states' rights. "Now," he said, "we are looking with terror at the great maelstrom of legislative misrule." Alluding to the advent of Congressional Reconstruction just a year earlier, Munford described "counties under the thralldom of military occupation, sending forth spawn, to rule and have dominion over her people!" His only hope was that one day, "if the constitution should ever be respected again [and] the olden times should ever return," it would protect "not only the rights of minorities," by which he meant southern whites, "but State rights."[1]

Munford's speech also reflected on Revolutionary War ancestors. Like many others after him, he expressed a belief that white southerners were the real defenders of the founders' legacy of liberty and insisted that Confederate soldiers were patriots cut from the same cloth. He asserted that secession was necessary to preserve states' rights, while northerners in Congress were "the chief violator[s] of the Constitution." According to Munford, the South had no choice but to go to war because its citizens were "threatened by violations of the constitution, and impending violations of the rights of property." That property, even though he did not give it a name, was slaves.[2]

Yet Munford's speech zeroed in on what became a central tenet of white southerners' postwar beliefs. The South's cause was a "holy cause," he proclaimed, and while "the Southern Confederacy has gone down never to rise . . . she will be like the sun when he sets—whose 'glory remains when his light fades away.'" He acknowledged defeat, but nothing more.

Munford also addressed the work of white southern women in defense and remembrance of the Confederacy. Men would not forget "the purity of our women, nor the sacrifices they made," he noted, but there was still work to do. It was a "duty" and "a debt of gratitude" that the white South "must pay." Munford was referring to the work of caring for the Confederate dead, a role fulfilled by women. "Our southern wives and daughters have inaugurated the undertaking. . . . They have collected the bones of the mighty dead," Munford explained, "and it is their purpose to beautify and adorn the place [Hollywood Cemetery] so that pilgrims may come to it as a modern Mecca."[3] He then exhorted others to help in what he described as "holy work."[4]

Holy cause. Holy work. Modern Mecca. Mary and Martha of the Bible represented yet another religious metaphor often used to describe the work of southern women whose care for the Confederate dead was seen as a demonstration of their faith and devotion. Later in the nineteenth century, white southerners extended the analogy of southern martyrdom so far that Confederate president Jefferson Davis would be likened to no less a figure than Jesus Christ. In effect, the religious language was critical to white southerners coming to terms with defeat, and it shaped the Lost Cause into what historian Charles Reagan Wilson has called the South's "civil religion."[5]

Southern women were inspired by this public calling couched in spiritual terms. Having stepped into the breach of war by providing for soldiers' needs and by caring for them in their local hospitals, southern women's lives had forever changed. They supported the war effort by forming soldiers' aid societies. According to one description, southern women during the war were "Florence Nightingales" and "tireless toilers whose needles were as flashing blades in battle."[6] Almost immediately after the war, they reorganized the soldiers' aid societies into ladies' memorial associations (or LMAs), and they were instrumental in shaping the Confederate tradition in the South in the decades that followed. The evidence of their work is visible in most southern communities, since they were the first to erect Confederate monuments in the region.

While the foundations for monument building across the South were originally based in bereavement and remembrance, the Confederate generation quickly infused monument dedications with a defiant Lost Cause rhetoric about the justness of secession, the superiority of southern civilization, and the necessity of preserving the racial status quo in the absence of slavery. Understanding the rituals of monument dedications and annual observances to the Confederate dead are critical to our knowledge of what these statues meant to many white southerners not only in the immediate aftermath of war but also going forward. Those committed to the

Lost Cause were, in essence, committed to a new form of southern nationalism that invoked white supremacy.

■ ■ ■

From their inception, ladies' memorial associations had both immediate objectives and long-term goals for memorializing the Confederate dead. The very first task they assumed was to oversee the return of bodies of dead Confederates from battlefields where they were buried back to hometown cemeteries. Though most had died on battlefields in the South, LMAs in various cities were especially eager to reinter the soldiers who had been buried at Gettysburg in Pennsylvania. In Charleston, South Carolina, for example, that process began during the war as soldiers who died in and around the city were buried in Magnolia Cemetery. Even in the midst of war, women cared for the graves of dead Confederates. According to an early history of the Ladies' Memorial Association of Charleston, the burials during the war "became the nucleus of a Confederate Cemetery," and the women already knew that their next step was to "erect a suitable monument to their [the soldiers'] memory."[7]

During the first two years after the war ended, the women of Charleston moved swiftly to honor those buried in Magnolia Cemetery. They raised $10,000 to erect headstones over each of the 800 graves and had enough left over to go toward a monument. This was the period known as Presidential Reconstruction, between 1865 and 1867, when Andrew Johnson had essentially given the South carte blanche to handle its postwar affairs, including the transition from slavery to freedom. And in the South Carolina legislature, described by the LMA in Charleston as "unreconstructed," representatives "came liberally to the aid of the Association, and gave one thousand dollars" to its work. The state also "granted the Association a large quantity of granite and marble," in part to complete the headstone project, but also for a monument.[8]

Yet by the time the LMA was to receive the material, the relationship between the South and the federal government shifted. Presidential Reconstruction was succeeded by what is known as Congressional Reconstruction, as the Republican-led Congress had begun to enforce compliance by states of the former Confederacy. Not only were federal troops occupying cities and towns in the South, but new governments were installed with leaders who would ensure laws were being followed. And they were not there to support Confederate memorialization.

Undaunted, southern women were determined to continue their memorialization efforts. Their goals were twofold. First, they sought to establish a memorial day for the annual decoration of graves. As Mrs. Charles J. Williams, secretary of the LMA in Columbus, Georgia, wrote, "We feel it is an unfinished work unless a day be set apart annually." Second, they planned to erect monuments in the Confederate section of their cemeteries.[9]

Reconstruction and accompanying federal occupation thwarted these women's efforts. The Charleston LMA knew that "those in charge . . . had not sympathy for the objects of [their] Association." The group's president, Mary Snowden, was persistent and successful in getting Governor Robert Scott, a Pennsylvanian and former Union general, to issue an order to deliver the granite "which the [prior] Legislature had granted." Mary and her sister Isabella were already well known in Charleston for their prewar work to raise a monument to John C. Calhoun, and they were credited with keeping those funds hidden during the war. Both women helped secure plats of land in Magnolia Cemetery for the burial of Confederate soldiers. Mary, in particular, took responsibility for returning the bodies of soldiers who fell at Gettysburg back to Charleston. Neither she nor her associates were going to accept that they could not do the work of memorialization, even in the face of federal occupiers.[10]

In Montgomery, Alabama, "during the distressing time of military rule," troops were said to have "hindered the work" of the LMA by suspending memorial activities, according to Ina Ockenden, who wrote a history of the group. In an account of the work of the Wake County LMA from Raleigh, North Carolina, the author claimed that federal troops in that city prohibited the members of the association from going to the cemetery in a procession and advised that if they did so, "they would be fired upon without further warning." Undeterred, the women formed pairs and eventually made it to the cemetery to place flowers and wreaths upon the graves while being "watched by a Federal officer to see that no procession was formed."[11] While women were able to create spaces within their local cemeteries for a monument, usually at the center of the graves of Confederate dead, actually erecting a monument was a step too far for occupying troops. Until federal forces were gone, women could not "raise monumental shafts."[12] For the time being, they began to commemorate what they called "Memorial Day," which eventually became known as Confederate Memorial Day. As one woman wrote, even "the veriest radical . . . could not refuse us the simple privilege of paying honor to those who died defending the life, honor, and happiness of Southern Women."[13]

LMAs in different towns declared the honor of being the "first" group of women to have founded this tradition. From Winchester, Virginia, to Columbus, Georgia, to Charleston, South Carolina, southern women lay claim to originating what some referred to as the "Sabbath of the South." Yet it seems clear that these spring rituals emerged more or less simultaneously throughout the region. Women in all of the states of the former Confederacy reinterred soldiers in their local cemeteries and marked their graves. They also set aside a specific day to annually decorate the graves. States in the Lower South settled on April 26, the day of General Joseph Johnston's surrender, while states in the Upper South chose May 10, the day General Thomas "Stonewall" Jackson died. Over time, these Confederate Memorial Days became significant events in communities and grew less somber and more celebratory as the Confederate tradition expanded.

■ ■ ■

Despite white southerners' frustration with Reconstruction and military occupation, neither lasted forever. Almost immediately after federal troops were withdrawn, southern women sought to make good on their promise to build monuments, first within the Confederate section of cemeteries where space had been re-served for that purpose, and soon after in highly visible public spaces in their communities. And while cemetery statues were relatively modest in design, LMAs seemed intent on making a statement on public landscapes—in the center of town or along a well-traveled boulevard—by raising monuments that involved long-range planning, enormous fundraising efforts, and design competitions.

They moved fast. In 1875, just four years after federal troops left the state, the LMA of Augusta, Georgia, laid the cornerstone for what became a seventy-six-foot-tall monument in the center of town. The Augusta Confederate monument is particularly instructive for understanding not only how southern communities expanded what it meant to commemorate fallen comrades but also how the Lost Cause became ritualized into a full-blown celebration of the Confederacy, its defenders, and white supremacy.

Augusta, located in the eastern part of the state, sits across the Savannah River from South Carolina, and before the Civil War it developed as a market town for short-staple cotton grown on surrounding plantations. During the war, Augusta's factories, including a Confederate powder works, supplied the southern army, while its railroads served to move supplies swiftly between eastern and western sections of the Confederacy. General William T. Sherman avoided Augusta on his famous March to the Sea, thinking it too well defended; subsequently, after the war, the town was in better economic shape than other southern towns and cities destroyed by Sherman's bummers. By 1872, conservative Democrats, known as "Redeemers," many of whom were former Confederate officers, were firmly in control of Georgia's state government. This left the door wide open for women in Augusta to begin their efforts to build a monument in earnest.[14]

Like other memorial efforts in the South, the Augusta LMA began by creating a soldiers' section in the city cemetery with a "foundation erected at the centre" for a monument, but the group was far more determined to erect "a marble shaft in some public place in the city" in memory of Richmond County's Confederate dead. Members advertised for designs, and Van Gunden, Young, and Grimm of Philadelphia won the contract with a bid of $500. It was one of many northern firms that capitalized on the monument-building fervor in the South throughout the late nineteenth and early twentieth centuries. Italy, too, reaped the benefits of Augusta's efforts, as the women purchased the marble to build the monument directly from Carrara. Monuments to the Lost Cause were, simply put, a lucrative business.[15]

For many monuments, including those in cemeteries, laying the cornerstone marked the first stage in the process of memorialization. The foundation alone could be costly. In New Bern, North Carolina, for example, the cornerstone of the cemetery statue was placed in 1867 at a cost of $2,000. The goal was always to erect a full monument on a foundation, but the fundraising for it could take time. In New Bern, it took eighteen years of collecting from "annual dues, festivals, concerts, mite chests, [and] donations" and a big advertising push in the columns of the local newspaper before there was enough money to build the eighteen-foot memorial. Such a time lapse happened more frequently in smaller towns, but in Augusta, the time between laying the cornerstone and building the monument was just three years.[16]

It cannot be overstated how quickly the Confederate tradition transformed after Reconstruction came to an end. There was more widespread involvement from the white community, and new rituals emerged. The LMAs continued to lead the charge to raise funds and build monuments while also determining how commemorative rituals would play out publicly, such that even placing the cornerstone for a monument came with its own ceremony, as the case of Augusta demonstrates. Just ten years after the end of the Civil War, in April 1875, locals witnessed more than a simple procession to Magnolia Cemetery to decorate the graves of Confederate dead with flowers. In that year, the white community reclaimed the town for the Lost Cause.

Military bands, veterans, the mayor, former Confederate officers, and leaders of the LMA led a procession through the center of town. The Augusta Volunteer Battalion, made up of several men who fought in the war, joined them, as did the Augusta police force, "armed with muskets, with fixed bayonets." The Schuetzen Club of German citizens, who wore "grey jackets and black pants and felt hats trimmed with green plumes," also added color to the parade. They marched toward the place on Broad Street where the cornerstone was to be laid and, as with monument unveilings before and after, listened to a speech from a Confederate veteran or political dignitary—who sometimes could be one and the same.[17]

An estimated 10,000 people attended the Augusta ceremonies in 1875. With local masons on hand to assist, women were literally involved in the laying of the cornerstone. The president of the memorial association was the first to take a trowel, dip it in mortar, and "[place] the first brick of the foundation of the monument." The *Constitutionalist* reported, "It was indeed a novel sight to the larger number of spectators to see the ladies, with delicate ungloved hands, laying brick and handling the trowel," noting that they had taken the first step in fulfilling their "holy duty" to erect "a shaft of marble in memory of the brave men who fought and died for a cause they considered just."[18]

Then came the day's speaker, General Clement Evans, a Civil War hero, Methodist minister, and Lost Cause stalwart who later headed the Georgia Division of the United Confederate Veterans. Evans's speech had many of the same elements of speeches given on Confederate Memorial Day and during monument unveilings. He articulated the South's anger over Reconstruction, lauded the work of southern women, linked the American Revolution to the Confederate cause, and remained defiant that secession was just. Only ten years had passed since the war ended, but for Evans and the thousands in attendance, the memory of those who sacrificed their lives was "as fresh and green as if it was only yesterday." He expressed optimism that "the long dispute between the Northern and Southern sections," which he estimated began fifty years earlier, were "practically drawing to a close." And despite four years of "fraternal carnage and its ten years aftermatter of crimination, distrust, and misrule"—a clear allusion to Reconstruction—he remained hopeful.[19]

Evans then moved on to speak about southern women, reminding the crowd that "we assemble at women's call—a call that men may gladly obey." It was common for men asked to give speeches during these ceremonies not only to compliment the women's work but also to assign them a special role within the Confederate tradition. "It is not man's privilege, but woman's to raise these memorials throughout the land," Evans said, adding that men must "yield to her the foremost place in this pleasing duty." In doing so, he placed southern women on a metaphoric pedestal for doing the work of building actual pedestals for monuments that honored Confederate soldiers like himself. Just as southern soldiers fulfilled their military duty, southern women now assumed the duty of honoring those men. The truth is, they were the only ones who could do it at the time, given that the veterans were certainly in no position to erect memorials after failing to win the war.[20]

Integral to the Lost Cause narrative was the belief that it was the Confederacy, not the Union, that had maintained the constitutional legacy of states' rights. Such rhetoric frequently made its way into monument speeches. Clement Evans alluded to these beliefs when he spoke. "I mean no boast, I only affirm that Southern ideas are still rooted in the old maxims of the first revolution," he claimed, "and they were not surrendered when the Confederate flag was furled, and Lee gave his sword to Grant." Evans's comments echo Edward Pollard in what the war had and had not settled, especially states' rights, and transformed rebels into patriots.[21]

Even as the former general told the assembled crowd that he advised against "[keeping] alive the passions of war," claiming that the "voice of the monument will not be for war, but peace," he asserted that "it was right to repel aggression. . . . It was right to set up a separate government. . . . It was right to hold out to the bitter end. Right! Right!" He also made a salient point about statues for those who wished to understand their meaning. "I have no doubt of the public utility of these monuments," he said, "[to] keep the popular heart drawn to the original principles and policies of this Government," concluding that "in common with others of like character which shall adorn every city of the South, this monument will mould and preserve Southern opinion." In other words, monuments were not simply commemorative; they represented the values and the "principles and policies" of states' rights and the preservation of white supremacy. Evans finally conceded that the Confederacy was dead. "We buried it. We do not intend to examine its remains. We were utterly defeated, and we dismiss our resentments." And yet his pronounced resentment very much underlay his message.[22]

Significantly, there were papers in the North that reprinted just those conciliatory parts of the speech. The *Burlington Free Press* in Vermont regarded the "ex-rebel General Evans" as having issued a call for reconciliation, while the *Pittsburgh Daily Post*, which received the entire speech over telegraph, selectively printed only those sentences that spoke of dismissing resentments and considering the monument as the "voice" of peace. "These are the sentiments of all the prominent Southern leaders who took part in the war," the paper noted. "It is time that we, too, had begun to forget the war," adding, "being the victors we ought to be more generous in this respect than the vanquished." In their reading of Evans's speech, northerners understood that *they* were the ones who should move on. Such columns were among the first to concede the memory of the war to southern interpretation.[23]

Not much had changed three years later, when the Augusta monument was unveiled in October 1878. An enormous crowd, estimated to be 20,000 people, was on hand for the dedication. Another parade ensued, this time with a cavalry regiment. Confederate flags were noticeably everywhere, carried by parade participants and hung from balconies on homes and local businesses. American flags were also flown during these and other Confederate commemorations, and not simply as a sign of reunification. To do so also symbolized that southerners saw themselves as loyal Americans who fought to defend constitutional principles, specifically states' rights. This was in keeping with the narrative that Confederates were the true inheritors of the American Revolution's legacy of patriotism. To that end in Augusta, a tall staff was placed on the platform in front of the monument "which waved a United States flag and a Confederate flag together." Placed across both flags was a white pennant bearing the word "Peace."[24]

The LMA tapped Charles Colcock Jones Jr. to speak. Jones, a lieutenant colonel in the Confederate army and former mayor of Savannah, began by addressing the work of women to erect the monument in memory of the soldiers from Richmond County who had died during the war. As he spoke to the enormous crowd, which included Georgia's governor, he was unrepentant in his defense of the Lost Cause. He reassured his fellow white southerners that they "have no apologies to offer, no excuses to render, no regrets to utter, save that we failed in our high endeavor." He then offered the well-worn excuse for defeat: "We were overborne by superior numbers and weightier munitions." Jones echoed Edward Pollard's pronouncement of twelve years earlier when he said, "Nothing has been absolutely determined except the question of comparative strength."[25]

Jones commented on the irony of the day's ceremonies, too, because the white citizens of Augusta were dedicating an elaborate monument memorializing those who were "overcome in the contest, to the cause which they seemingly lost." Significantly, he used the word "overcome" rather than "defeated," but even more noteworthy was his suggestion that all had *not* been lost. He also believed that the day was coming when anyone "with the candor to confess," even northerners, would acknowledge the Confederacy was right in its fight for an "independent national existence." Last, he hinted at what became a key component of the Lost Cause—indoctrinating southern children—noting that children should "be taught to emulate the example of their Confederate ancestors."[26]

A member of the LMA unveiled the monument, and the women asked that their fellow white citizens "cooperate" by joining them annually in commemoration of Confederate Memorial Day by decorating both the graves of soldiers and the new statue with flowers. They thanked the local paper, the *Constitutionalist*, for its valuable assistance to their fundraising efforts. And those efforts were significant, as the total cost for the design, material, supplies, and sculpture came to more than $17,000, a value of nearly $433,000 in 2020.[27]

As the case of Augusta shows, post-Reconstruction monument building became a public enterprise that moved the Confederate tradition from mourning into the realm of celebration. No longer limited to decorating the graves of soldiers on Confederate Memorial Day, that annual ritual now included a stop at the monument to pay homage to a mythologized past. It also demonstrates how entrenched the Lost Cause narrative had become, with its emphasis on a just cause and a sacred duty to Confederate principles, such that going forward it also included a commitment to perpetuate a false history among coming generations of white children in the South.

■ ■ ■

The Augusta monument marked a trend in monument building in the following decades, not only in terms of its size, cost, and placement but in its glorification of Confederate general Robert E. Lee in particular. While the centerpiece of the town's monument was a soldier atop a tall column, around its base were individual figures honoring local heroes and also one of Lee, who swiftly became the white South's most celebrated and commemorated hero, especially after his death in 1870 and despite his opposition to postwar monument building.

More than once, Lee made his feelings clear that Confederate markers and statues were antithetical to a peaceful reconciliation. In 1866, he avoided supporting a monument proposal, writing, "All I think that can now be done, is to aid our noble & generous women in their efforts to protect the graves & mark the last resting places of those who have fallen, & wait for better times." A few years later, in response to a proposed monument at Gettysburg, Lee reiterated his stance: "I think it wiser . . . not to keep open the sores of war, but to follow the examples of those nations who endeavored to obliterate the marks of civil strife, to commit to oblivion the feelings engendered." In many ways, his sentiments did not matter, even to the very same white southerners who held him in such high esteem. The Lost Cause did not belong to Lee; Lee belonged to the Lost Cause—a cultural phenomenon whose momentum could not be stopped.[28]

The shift toward building monuments to honor Robert E. Lee signaled important changes in the movement during the post-Reconstruction years. Since the end of the war, women had assumed responsibility for commemorating the Confederate dead; men encouraged it and, in some instances, designated it as being the exclusive domain of women. But when white men reassumed control over local and state governments, these "Redeemers" appeared more willing to play a leading role in commemoration. Many of them were former Confederate veterans who had been emasculated by defeat, but a dozen years after the war they augmented women's efforts by forming their own associations. The Lost Cause had now become a celebration of heroes in which they could see themselves playing an active role in restoring their own reputations.

In the year of Lee's death, 1870, two major southern cities, New Orleans and Richmond, each initiated a call to raise a monument to commemorate Lee. And in the year Reconstruction officially ended, 1877, both formed fundraising groups, the Robert E. Lee

Monument Association in New Orleans and the Lee Monument Association in Richmond. The plans in both cities were to build the grandest possible monument to Lee, and while funds for the New Orleans monument came directly from the immediate community, funding in Richmond became a multistate effort. Both campaigns illustrate how the regional fervor for the Lost Cause was matched only by the moneys that were spent in the effort.

As in other cities and towns throughout the South, New Orleans's first Confederate monument was intended to honor the dead. Women who had provided for their state's soldiers during the war reorganized as a memorial association in 1866. They first called themselves the Ladies' Confederate Memorial Association and intended to provide "suitable graves" for soldiers who died during the war. But because New Orleans was under federal occupation, the women were required to change the name of their group. According to General Philip Sheridan, the officer in charge, he could not "permit the flaunting of the word 'Confederate,'" so they renamed their group the Ladies' Benevolent Association.[29]

Over the course of eight years, from 1866 to 1874, the women's association raised nearly $30,000, the largest gift coming from the Princeton, New Jersey–born philanthropist Paul Tulane, who had also used his wealth to support the Confederate war effort. While most of the money went to assist indigent veterans and their families, the benevolent association directed more than $11,000 of the remaining funds to place a monument in Greenwood Cemetery. Unveiled on April 10, 1874, to little fanfare, the local press reported, "It was simple enough, and for that reason the more appropriate and more touching."[30]

Although a group of men formed the Robert E. Lee Monument Association in 1870, their work did not begin in earnest until federal troops—who had occupied the city since 1862—had completely withdrawn, in 1877. The association swiftly raised $10,000 for the statue of Lee, but the remaining elements of the structure—the mound, the pyramid of steps, and the marble column—were even more costly, so the fundraising continued. Regardless, the group hired the twenty-six-year-old sculptor Alexander Doyle from New York, whom the *New Orleans Times-Democrat* described as "a gentleman of fine physique [with] a handsome, manly face of the blonde order." In other words, a perfect Anglo-Saxon specimen of a man was chosen to create the "heroic figure of Lee."[31]

In the seven years after Doyle was hired, the remainder of the costs of the monument was raised. On February 7, 1884, New Orleanians learned that the bronze statue, cast by Henry and Bonnard Manufacturing of New York, had been shipped. The monument association announced it was offering souvenir medals for sale in stores throughout the city. Sales of the medals, embossed with an image of the Lee statue, were used to pay the final balance on the monument. The association then chose February 22 for the unveiling. Unveiling dates were often symbolic and aligned with other important dates in history, and in this case, it was George Washington's birthday. It was a busy time in the city, too. Carnival season was in full swing, and the city was also preparing for the World's Industrial and Cotton Centennial Exposition.[32]

At the unveiling, seats had been provided for between 3,000 and 4,000 people, which the press noted was insufficient to accommodate a crowd that was easily four times that in size. Not only was the area around the monument congested, but so were the streets that radiated from the circle of land on which it sat. The dignitaries at the unveiling ceremony were a who's who of the Confederate South. Jefferson Davis appeared with his daughters, while Lee's daughters Mary and Mildred Lee represented the general's family. Members of the monument association, chief among them the celebrated Confederate general P. G. T. Beauregard, were prominent, as were an entire cavalcade of state officeholders. The governor, senators, and members of the state supreme court attended, and similar to ceremonies in Augusta six years earlier, a parade included militias, a band, and a 100-gun salute.[33]

Just as the time arrived for the unveiling, a great torrent of rain and wind dispersed the crowd, but during a brief respite they returned to watch Jefferson Davis perform the honor of pulling the cord that sent the fabric covering the monument cascading down to its foundation, revealing it publicly for the first time. Confederate soldiers roared with approval, as did members of the Grand Army of the Republic, described by the *Daily Picayune* as having "cast up their hate as enthusiastically as the men who wore the

The unveiling of the Robert E. Lee monument in New Orleans
in 1884 signaled a rededication to Confederate principles in the post-
Reconstruction South. Hundreds of children form a "living battle flag"
in front of the monument, symbolizing a future commitment
to the values of the Lost Cause.
(Courtesy of the Historic New Orleans Collection, 2012.0208.2.198)

gray." Northern veterans were not normally in attendance at such commemorations; that they were and that they joined Confederates in celebrating a monument to Lee proved an early sign that white northerners were softening to the spirit of the Lost Cause.[34]

In describing the events of the day, nearly twenty years after the Civil War ended, the *Daily Picayune* editorialized, "We cannot ignore the fact that the secession has been stigmatized as treason," an aspersion cast upon the South that, in the newspaper's view, should be rejected. The paper further expressed the new defiance that the Lost Cause came to represent in the years after Reconstruction: "We must show to all coming ages that with us, at least, there dwells no sense of guilt."[35]

When all was said and done, the monument to Robert E. Lee in New Orleans rose 109 feet. The bronze figure of Lee alone stood 16 feet tall and was hailed at the time as "the largest bronze statue ever cast in New York." The cost of the monument, including the $10,000 paid to the sculptor, came to $36,474—an estimated $945,000 in 2020.[36]

■ ■ ■

Richmond was not to be outdone in the contest to build the grandest monument to Lee in the South, but the infighting among men and women over design, funding, and placement delayed that effort another six years after the dedication of the New Orleans monument. Following Lee's death in 1870, the white South's eagerness to honor him was especially intense in his home state of Virginia. Lee's character and military reputation among white southerners was unassailable, and he came to symbolize all that was noble about the southern cause—and, by association, all Confederate veterans. For men, especially, erecting a grand monument to Lee as the Lost Cause hero par excellence was seen as an opportunity to restore their own honor, as well as to erase any remaining residue of shame and emasculation caused by defeat. As such, the monument needed to reflect both his and their own importance to the region in scale and design.

Initial calls to create an equestrian statue of the general emerged among veterans in Lexington, where Lee last lived. Eventually, however, the momentum to build the statue resided in Richmond. The Lee Monument Association was headed by former Confederate general Jubal Early, who considered himself the leader of the movement to honor Lee. Certainly aware of how critical women's efforts had been to Confederate memorialization, he invited the Hollywood Memorial Association to "assist." Yet the Confederate tradition had long been dominated by women in Virginia, and they were not simply going to hand over the reins to the men. Serving as helpmeet was an unacceptable proposition, especially to the association's leader, Sarah Randolph, who descended from prominent Virginians. While on the surface the women appeared to back the men's monument group and reorganized themselves as the Ladies' Lee Monument Committee, in reality their experience made the difference in how events unfolded in Richmond. They raised the most money, they controlled the purse strings, and in the end, under Randolph's leadership, the committee selected the design and sculptor. In the long battle for control over the Lee monument, the women were the victors.[37]

The unveiling was scheduled for May 29, 1890, and on May 25 the *Richmond Dispatch* announced a three-day schedule of events that included "Parades, Ceremonies, Addresses, Balls, and Other Entertainments." Wednesday before the unveiling would include a Memorial Day observance in the Hebrew cemetery, a military ball and reception, and a choral performance by the Young Men's Christian Association. In addition to a reunion of Confederate cavalry veterans, Thursday—the day of the unveiling—plans included a "parade of veterans, volunteers, civic societies, and [the] fire department." Later that evening, a fireworks display was arranged. On Friday, May 30, Memorial Day observances were scheduled in Hollywood Cemetery to feature addresses by governors from Virginia, West Virginia, and Florida. The names of guests from around the country, especially notable veterans from throughout the South, were listed in the *Dispatch* in alphabetical order and took up most of the front page.[38]

The city of Richmond had worked up to the last minute to prepare for the onslaught of people in town for the unveiling of the massive statue of Lee on his horse Traveler. Monument unveilings, while initially few in number immediately after the war, had become celebrated events in the life of southern communities since Reconstruction, but they all paled in comparison to events in Richmond. On the day of the unveiling, an estimated crowd of 100,000 people surrounded the platform and spilled down the streets as they eagerly awaited the moment white southerners everywhere had long anticipated. The grand statue of their hero was unveiled, the crowd roared in approval, and there, on stands built adjacent to this soaring figure, were hundreds of white children wearing clothing in red, white, and blue, arranged in the shape of a "living" Confederate battle flag. It was a harbinger of Lost Cause traditions.

The celebrations that took place throughout the city prior to and during the unveiling revealed how far the Lost Cause had come in twenty-five years. This was not just a monument to the region's most cherished hero; it was about the restoration of Confederate men's honor. The *Richmond Times* said as much in its editorial "Conquered Though Not Vanquished." Reflecting on this historic moment in the city, the editor mused that "in the character of Robert E. Lee, the Southern civilization had attained its most consummate expression." Lee's character had a "tenacious hold upon the southern people," the *Times* asserted. "He is not merely the exponent of a cause that has perished"; rather, Lee's character represented "lofty traits" in which white southerners could take pride "as the highest expression of their own aggregate greatness."[39]

What happened in Richmond in May 1890 was emblematic of how the Confederacy's defeat had transformed into something new in the haze of historical amnesia and Lost Cause rhetoric. It also signaled to those in attendance, both veterans and the generation of white southerners born since the war, that the lawful changes made possible by Reconstruction no longer had meaning. The rights of black citizens, in fact, were slowly being destroyed, and in the decade to come, elimination of those rights would be completed through both legal and extralegal means. The decade of the 1890s also marked a new phase in the Confederate tradition, one led by a new organization of women and that expanded beyond celebration, calling for complete vindication of the Lost Cause and the Confederate generation.

■ ■ ■

Three decades after the Civil War, white southerners continued their efforts to commemorate the Lost Cause, but between 1890 and World War I those efforts assumed a different tone and new intensity. Monument building, in particular, expanded to nearly every town and hamlet throughout the South and now appeared on courthouse lawns, in town squares, and on the grounds of state government. Commemoration took many forms. Highways were named for Robert E. Lee and even Jefferson Davis, and images of these same men were cast into the stained glass windows of churches. Confederate Memorial Day became an official state holiday in southern states, too, but monuments continued to be the most visible and tangible reminders of the Lost Cause and the white South's unceasing loyalty to the principle of states' rights, which in the late nineteenth and early twentieth centuries meant the right to maintain a system of segregation based in white supremacy.

The 1890s were also a decade marked by the disfranchisement of black men across the region. Southern states had long rejected the idea of black citizenship, but during this decade they amped up their efforts to eliminate it altogether. While southern legislatures passed laws that reversed voting rights, white men across the region used racial violence, especially lynching, not only to intimidate black voters but to subdue entire black communities. The result was that by the turn of the twentieth century, black men, even those who once served in Congress, were prohibited from voting and holding office. This left a vacancy in the southern polity, and southern white women assumed an even more public role as leaders of the Confederate tradition. When they did, it was primarily through the United Daughters of the Confederacy, which became the most influential southern women's organization for the next several decades.

During a decade that saw the rise of women's clubs and ancestral societies, the UDC became extremely popular with women across the region, and its ranks grew exponentially after its founding in 1894. The growth in monument building paralleled the growth of the UDC's membership, since the Daughters were primarily responsible for the vast majority of monuments and memorials built throughout the South, and even beyond its borders, during those years. The period between the mid-1890s and World War I represents the peak period of monument dedications and demonstrates how seriously these southern white women took their role as leaders of the Lost Cause. The mark they made on the social, political, and physical landscape of the region in the early twentieth century is undeniable, such that the term "New South" is practically a misnomer.

The Daughters' heightened visibility and their broader agenda to cement a loyalty to Confederate principles among future generations of white southerners provided the cultural foundation upon which rested the white supremacist legislation created by their male counterparts throughout the South. This was not a coincidence, since southern white women not only shared similar views on racial supremacy but were also related by blood or marriage to men of influence within the region, from local attorneys and judges to governors and state legislators.[40]

Women who rose to the rank of president-general of the UDC included the daughters of Confederate generals and U.S. congressmen, and in Mississippi, two of the early presidents of the organization were daughters of U.S. senators. One was Lizzie George Henderson, whose father, James Z. George, authored the 1890 "Mississippi Plan." She shared her father's views on race and inherited his leadership skills, rising through the ranks of the UDC to become its president-general from 1905 to 1907. She once bragged that in her hometown of Greenwood, Mississippi, local members of the UDC's J. Z. George Chapter, named after her father, placed framed copies of the state's secession ordinance in the white public schools. She also led efforts to erect a Confederate monument on the grounds of Leflore County Courthouse and to construct the Confederate Memorial Building in town that contained a library of pro-southern texts.[41]

The Daughters were motivated not just to honor their veteran ancestors but to vindicate them as well, a term they used repeatedly in their writings. While funding monuments and memorials and lobbying for their placement were critical aspects of their work in the early twentieth century, their agenda looked toward the future as much as it commemorated the past. UDC members sought to ensure that future generations of white southerners would also hold up their Confederate ancestors as heroes and would themselves become defenders of the same principles for which their ancestors fought and died, including a staunch defense of states' rights.

The UDC did so through a multipronged approach. In addition to raising the money to build the hundreds of monuments and memorials that dot the southern and national landscape, members' objectives included preserving and perpetuating the "true," albeit revisionist, history of slavery, the Confederate cause, and Reconstruction. The women also lobbied state legislatures to provide pensions to Confederate veterans and to build homes for Confederate soldiers and their widows. They even expanded their influence over public education by helping teachers develop lesson plans, monitoring textbooks, placing battle flags and portraits of Confederate generals in classrooms, and forming groups of the Children of the Confederacy. In sum, they offered a robust defense of the Lost Cause that, in many ways, is still with us to this day.[42]

Of course, the most visible reminders of the Daughters' influence in the region are the monuments they erected in cemeteries and town squares, on the grounds of local and state courthouses, on national battlefields, in Arlington National Cemetery, and even at the United States Capitol. The equivalent of millions of dollars has been spent in this endeavor, some of which came through state and local government expenditures and involved an alliance between elected officials and the UDC. This alliance served to further protect the racial status quo.

That the majority of these monuments were built some thirty to fifty years after the Civil War and that so many were placed on sites of local and state government indicate that these statues were not simply works of public art or about honoring the dead; their larger purpose was to signal that white men were firmly in control of the southern legal system, the same system that disfranchised black voters and enforced Jim Crow legislation. And regardless of their artistic significance, monuments were intentional because white southerners regarded them as object lessons for future generations about the Confederate past and also about racial superiority.

Southern monuments were always supported by a narrative that Confederate veterans fought nobly and that defeat did not erase the justness of their cause. They were also a reflection of beliefs held by the Jim Crow generation—whites who regarded African Americans as second-class citizens and whose leaders sought to maintain their supremacy through legislation. And if there were any doubts about the larger meaning and purpose of Confederate monuments within the context of the Lost Cause, the Daughters made it clear in the minutes of their meetings, the essays they wrote, the speeches they gave, and the actions they took. Moreover, the men they selected to give speeches at monument unveilings, while they reiterated the message of honor and sacrifice, also furthered the Lost Cause narrative about slavery, the war, and Confederate soldiers as valiant heroes who not only fought to defend the South against an invading North but who withstood Reconstruction and became stalwart defenders of white supremacy, including as members of the Ku Klux Klan.

While the Daughters expanded the Confederate tradition, they remained committed to the work begun by their predecessors in ladies' memorial associations. Some members of LMAs simply joined the UDC, which brought together two generations of Lost Cause women. And in the early years following the UDC's founding, both groups could be found working together to raise money for monuments in their communities, although eventually the Daughters superseded memorial associations in influence across the South. This transfer of cultural power was evident at the unveiling of the Confederate monument in Montgomery, Alabama, in 1898.

The Montgomery monument was thirty years in the making, after a committee of men was incorporated in 1865 with the goal of locating a monument on the highest ground in the city adjacent to the state capitol, where "a nation was born." The local LMA, previously organized to mark the graves of Confederate soldiers, had through various fundraising events already erected a statue in the city cemetery. Members had leftover funds to go toward the monument on Capitol Hill, but it was not their project. As had happened in Virginia with the Lee monument, the all-male monument committee had made painfully slow progress, although members managed to pay for the creation of a foundation and invited the South's former chieftain, Jefferson Davis, to assist in laying the cornerstone on April 26, 1886, Confederate Memorial Day in Alabama. But right after the ceremonies, the men's monument association did what others like it had done—it handed over responsibility to the LMA, "realizing that memorial work belonged peculiarly to women." From that point forward, the women expanded their fundraising efforts and a committee from the group "haunted the legislative halls of the State" seeking money for the monument. When it was unveiled, at a cost of $45,000, it was considered to be "partly the gift of the State . . . a tribute by a generation that is here, to a generation that has gone."[43]

The LMA was joined in its fundraising by two new chapters of the UDC in Montgomery, which were formed in 1896 and 1897, respectively. The city was large enough to have more than one chapter, plus the LMA, whose membership numbered nearly 500. During dedication ceremonies, in fact, the Daughters held a place of prominence on the unveiling platform. Just a year earlier, the Sophie Bibb Chapter of the UDC placed a six-pointed brass star on the Capitol Building's west portico, marking the place where Jefferson Davis took his oath of office to become the Confederate president. In many ways, the monument unveiling symbolized the passing of the torch of the Confederate tradition to the next generation.

Thomas Jones, a major in the Confederate army and governor of Alabama from 1890 to 1894, was one of the special speakers of the day, and his words were those heard at Lost Cause ceremonies since 1865. He denied that the Civil War had been "fought over the justice or morality of slavery," emphasized that the North's superior numbers and material sources were the reasons for defeat, and offered a dramatic critique of Reconstruction. After Lee's surrender, he told the crowd, "the weary soldier put aside his thought of vengeance and trudged home," where "he found the slave his political master." During that time, Jones complained, the rights of states were "dead for twelve long years."[44]

Jones then turned his attention to the monument itself, proclaiming that providing a written history that exonerated the Confederacy was the important next step, since "our duty is not ended with the building of this monument." While he believed in the power of the statue to convey history and regarded it as a symbol to "stimulate youths to admire and to . . . emulate [if not] surpass the famous deeds" of their ancestors, he pressed for a written history to do the same. His words were echoed by another speaker that day, Hilary Herbert, President Grover Cleveland's secretary of the U.S. Navy. Herbert, who had served as a colonel in the Eighth Alabama infantry, spoke to the Montgomery crowd about the necessity of commemorative statues. "We build monuments to heroes," he said, so "that future generations may imitate their [Confederate soldiers'] example," adding that the monument before them would function to "keep . . . alive forever the glorious principles of liberty" for future generations.[45]

The United Daughters of the Confederacy had already heeded Herbert's call to "keep alive" the memory of the Confederate generation and teach future generations about the significance of states' rights to the southern cause, what Herbert called "principles of liberty." Since the organization's founding, members affirmed the instruction of children as one of their primary goals. If taught properly, they reasoned, then white children would grow up to become "living monuments" of the Lost Cause. The metaphor of a monument was purposeful. UDC members understood that they were leaders of the region's efforts to build statues of marble and bronze and remained dedicated to that purpose, yet they were also keenly aware that the most enduring monument to the Confederacy was a population of white southerners educated to defend both the memory and the principles for which it stood.[46]

Nonetheless, in the first two decades of the twentieth century, the UDC built monuments at a blazing pace. Between 1900 and 1910, they erected nearly 200, an average of 20 per year. The peak year of monument building was 1911, when the Daughters erected 48 monuments, an average of 4 every month. Then, between 1910 and 1920, the UDC dedicated an additional 205 statues. They did so even as the general organization completed fundraising and erected significant regional monuments, including the one honoring Jefferson Davis on Monument Avenue in Richmond in 1907 at a cost of $70,000; the Confederate monument in Arlington National Cemetery in 1914, which cost approximately $64,000; and the $50,000 monument at Shiloh National Military Park that was unveiled in 1917. In today's currency, the Daughters spent millions of dollars on these projects, significant sums of which were appropriated from state and local governments. Notably, this does not take into consideration the money spent on the numerous battlefield markers and other types of memorials these women also dedicated during these same years.[47]

The financial beneficiaries of this monument frenzy were not only the sculptors who won the UDC's design competitions but also businesses located in the North, the South, and even Europe. Bronze works in New York and Chicago advertised in the *Confederate Veteran* touting their designs and products, as did stone quarries in the South. The best known was the McNeel Marble Company in Marietta, Georgia, which advertised regularly in the *Confederate Veteran* as "The Largest Monumental Dealers in the South." In one ad from 1913, the company touted that it was completing several orders for monuments being dedicated in Arkansas, Florida, Georgia, Louisiana, North Carolina, Texas, and Virginia and reminded UDC chapters that time was of the essence, "so the old heroes of the sixties can enjoy" a monument honoring them "before it is too late."[48] The ad tapped into the sense of urgency across the region to honor veterans whose numbers were rapidly dwindling.

There were also fundraising efforts, led by men, to raise monuments dedicated to the women of the Confederacy, several of which were placed on the grounds of state capitols, such as those in Mississippi and North Carolina. In 1908, Caroline Goodlett told the women of the organization she had cofounded fourteen years earlier that she kept hoping that "the monument fever would abate." For her, the more important work was education, not "the stone and mortar business." While the Daughters heeded her call and established a committee on education, their "monument fever" only grew worse.[49]

While there was evidence that monument building was beginning to decelerate in the second decade of the new century, as fundraising in local communities slowed and monuments were taking longer to be completed, World War I interrupted even these efforts. The UDC completed most of the projects it had signed onto prior to the war except for Stone Mountain, which had been mired in controversy and false starts since it was first suggested in

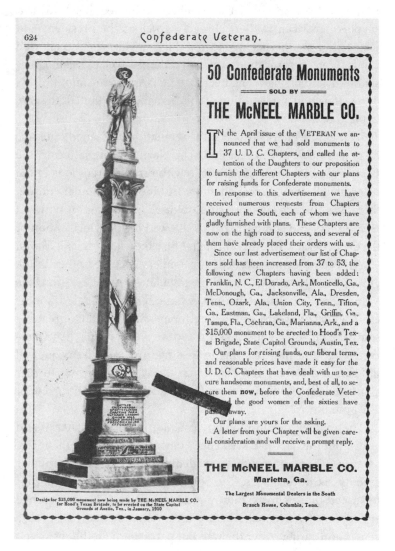

The McNeel Marble Company of Marietta, Georgia, targeted its advertisements to Confederate heritage groups, especially the UDC, as it sought to profit from the monument boom of the early twentieth century.
(*Confederate Veteran*, March 1909; courtesy Archive.org)

1916. More importantly, by the time the United States entered the First World War in 1917, UDC members redirected their efforts to support American soldiers abroad, as well as the president and their fellow southerner, Woodrow Wilson. The war also allowed Confederate organizations to revive the Lost Cause claim that southern soldiers had long been patriotic Americans, not traitors or rebels, as a new generation of southern men committed to serve in the U.S. military.

By the time of World War I, the reputation of Confederate soldiers had nearly been restored. The North's capitulation to the Lost Cause narrative, which began with veterans' reunions in the 1880s, had hastened reconciliation. In American popular culture, there was further evidence of a cultural reconciliation between northerners and southerners that allowed for the glorification of the Confederacy, whether through films like *The Birth of a Nation* (1915), where former Confederate soldiers become heroes in the guise of the Ku Klux Klan, or in popular songs like "The Dixie Volunteers," published in 1917, whose lyrics compared southern soldiers to their Confederate forebears. "See those great big southern lad-dies / just like their dear old dad-dies," the chorus went, "and they're going to be / fighting men like Stonewall Jackson and Robert E. Lee." It was the vindication that former Confederates and their descendants had wanted since surrender at Appomattox.[50]

The momentum in monument building renewed after World War I, but the pace had slackened considerably. During the 1920s, seventy-five monuments were dedicated, along with another seventy-six in the 1930s. The Second World War once again interrupted those efforts, but by then memories of a war that had ended seventy-five years before meant less than it had even a generation earlier. After the war, but particularly in the 1950s and early 1960s, there was a renewed interest in Confederate memory and monument building, especially as the Civil War centennial approached. Those decades also marked enormous changes to the southern way of life, as the civil rights movement challenged the political system that had kept black southerners from enjoying the full rights of citizenship. Somewhere in the midst of these competing developments, the monuments of Jim Crow remained, not as symbols of a long dead culture but as daily reminders of racial inequality.

CODA

On Confederate Memorial Day in North Carolina, May 10, 1933, Justice Heriot Clarkson of the state supreme court delivered an address to the Johnston Pettigrew Chapter of the United Daughters of the Confederacy in Raleigh. Standing in Oakwood Cemetery, alongside the Confederate monument erected by the ladies' memorial association, Clarkson began his speech by extolling the character of General Robert E. Lee as a model of Christian manhood and then sang the praises of General Thomas "Stonewall" Jackson's actions at the Battle of Manassas.[51]

After this very brief beginning, Clarkson's tone grew dark as he spoke about the "men who laid down their arms, and of the women of the South . . . [who] suffered as no others." He launched into a harangue on the "Tragic Era" of Reconstruction, when "carpetbaggers and scalawags, like the Egyptian locust, overran this fair land." When "millions of negro slaves were turned loose on the prostrate white race," he claimed, "these political vultures with the illiterate negro ruled the South." The result, in his estimation, and without a hint of irony, was that "Confederate soldiers were disfranchised" and "no race of people on this earth suffered more." Not even the enslaved population of the South.[52]

Clarkson's speech brightened, however, when he spoke of how white North Carolinians restored racial order in their government "founded on 'White Supremacy through white men.'" He specifically pointed to the 1899 general assembly in which a Democratic majority drafted the constitutional amendment that repudiated universal male suffrage, especially black suffrage, and "eliminated the illiterate." Then Clarkson softened, telling the Daughters that "when we look back at the crucifixion of the South, let us try to forgive and forget." It had taken sixty-eight years after the war for the South Carolina–born Clarkson, whose father had been a Confederate officer, to suggest that the white South could now express forgiveness for Reconstruction. He could do so because of what had been accomplished in his lifetime. "When the Anglo Saxon race gained supremacy in 1899," he recalled, "it was a turning point in this Commonwealth." For this, Clarkson believed, "it [was] a beautiful picture for all our people to look upon, both white and black."[53]

Yet the portrait Clarkson painted for his audience, including UDC members who likely nodded their approval, was one of a southern state that embedded white supremacy within its constitution at the dawn of a new century. His speech was unapologetic and expressed no regret about the disfranchisement of an entire race of people, even as a member of the highest court in North Carolina. While Clarkson's address undoubtedly pleased those gathered around the Confederate monument that day in 1933, it sent a message to African Americans that the doors of citizenship in the state where they made their home remained closed to them. Soon enough, they would begin to knock on those doors.

3

CONFEDERATE CULTURE AND THE STRUGGLE FOR CIVIL RIGHTS

On September 19, 1955, inside the Tallahatchie courthouse in Sumner, Mississippi, the trial for the murder of fourteen-year-old Emmett Till got under way. Black and white locals, as well as journalists from across the country, filled the courtroom to capacity. On each of the trial's five days, those unable to find seats inside gathered on the courthouse lawn. On the second day, the *Jackson Clarion-Ledger* reported, "Today, among about 100 outside, were 10 Negroes sitting at the base of a Confederate monument to Sumner's Civil War dead," while local whites took refuge in the shade of nearby trees.[1]

The story of the trial is well known, as are the events that followed. Roy Bryant and J. W. Milam, who were later paid for an interview with *Look* magazine in which they confessed to the

During the Emmett Till murder trial in Sumner, Mississippi, in 1955, the courtroom was always filled to capacity. Trial observers spilled onto the courthouse grounds. Local blacks were left to sit on the steps to the Confederate monument, while local whites took refuge from the heat in the shade of courthouse trees.

(Courtesy of the Archives and Records Services Division, Mississippi Division of Archives and History) murder, were acquitted by an all-white male jury only a few days later. The horrific details of Till's killing—retribution for breaking southern social taboos by talking "fresh" to a white woman—combined with the obvious injustice of the trial are often credited with launching the modern civil rights movement. Only a few months after the murder, Rosa Parks was arrested and jailed for refusing to move from her seat on a Montgomery city bus. As she recalled, "I thought of Emmett Till and when the bus driver ordered me to move to the back, I just couldn't move."[2]

The description of African Americans sitting around the base of the Confederate statue on the grounds of the Tallahatchie courthouse during Till's trial was an unremarkable detail, little reported in its time—and yet it functioned as a powerful metaphor for the racial injustice taking place inside. Segregated even on the courthouse grounds, local whites took refuge from the Delta heat beneath courthouse trees, while black citizens were left to rest in the shadow of the Confederate monument whose placement adjacent to a court of law stood as a sharp rebuke of justice for African Americans. And yet their presence, as they simply sat around the monument's base, was an important demonstration of their investment in the trial's outcome.

Decades earlier, the Tallahatchie County Board of Supervisors, as a testament to its commitment to the Lost Cause, had approved $1,000 of taxpayer money as its portion of the monument's cost, which the United Daughters of the Confederacy dedicated in 1913.[3] On one side of the pedestal, the words "Our Heroes" are inscribed, while another side is etched with a poem, the last line of which reads, "They left the cause that never yet has failed." Some of those "heroes" became avowed white supremacists after the war, and their progeny reversed the gains of Reconstruction as they established Jim Crow in its wake. The poem on the monument also expressed the local white community's continued belief in the Confederate cause, not as a failed cause but a just one that was still ongoing. By 1913, however, preserving white supremacy and segregation had become the "cause." Several decades later, as the outcome of the Emmett Till murder trial proved, it remained true. And Tallahatchie's Confederate monument, just like the hundreds of others located on courthouse grounds throughout the South, stood as a stone sentinel to white supremacy.

By the mid-twentieth century, both the Lost Cause and the protests against it had taken on a new tone. Southern whites continued to venerate the Confederate tradition, particularly in light of a burgeoning civil rights movement, as they held fast to ideas of states' rights and the racial status quo. Likewise, black resistance to the Lost Cause was present and could take different forms. In the 1950s and 1960s, such resistance might appear as public critique of the Confederate battle flag, but it also directly challenged the message of Confederate monuments, as civil rights marches often coalesced around the statues that dominated town squares or courthouse lawns. There, next to Johnny Reb, speeches about racial equality, rather than Lost Cause platitudes, were heard, as a movement gathered strength to reclaim the public square for all citizens.

■ ■ ■

Criticism of the Lost Cause and Confederate symbols stretched back as early as 1870, when Frederick Douglass called out the "*nauseating* flatteries of the late Robert E. Lee" that poured in after the Confederate general's death, asking, "Is it not about time that this bombastic laudation of the rebel chief should cease?"[4] Until his death in 1895, Douglass engaged in an uphill battle to dislodge the Lost Cause narrative that had gripped the national consciousness while still seeking to preserve the memory of emancipation. But the pull of the Lost Cause was strong. Even white northerners were willing to make a devil's bargain with the South's Confederate tradition for the sake of sectional reconciliation. And the race to build "monuments of folly," as Douglass called them, had yet to peak by the time of his death.[5]

Still, while Frederick Douglass waged a battle against the North's capitulation to the Lost Cause the rest of his life, the real war against it was in the South, where black southerners were on the front lines. They were keenly aware that Confederate symbols in their communities were imbued with racism and white supremacy, and they protested them publicly and privately. Some of the earliest identifiable southern protests occurred in Charleston, South Carolina, in response to the monument built to honor

John C. Calhoun, U.S. senator, secretary of war, and vice president of the United States from 1825 to 1832. Calhoun was also a fierce defender of states' rights to preserve the institution of slavery. While not technically a Confederate monument—Calhoun died in 1850, long before the South seceded—its unveiling on April 26, 1887, Confederate Memorial Day in South Carolina, and the ceremonies that accompanied it, including the singing of "Dixie," placed it firmly in the Lost Cause tradition.

From the outset, the Calhoun monument, centrally located on the Citadel Green, was the object of derision within the local black community. As historians Ethan J. Kytle and Blain Roberts have shown, black Charlestonians "mocked and vandalized the monument," as did some white Charlestonians, but for different reasons: whites reviled it for its aesthetics, while African Americans despised it because of what Calhoun represented to their race. As Mamie Garvin Fields, a black Charlestonian born in 1888, put it, "Since we thought like [Frederick] Douglass, we hated all that Calhoun stood for." The monument, therefore, was more than an irritant. According to Fields, "Blacks took that statue personally," because it was as if Calhoun was speaking to them, telling them, "Nigger, you may not be a slave, but I am back to see you stay in your place." And they responded to its hateful message. "We used to carry something with us, if we knew we would be passing that way, in order to deface that statue—scratch up the coat, break the watch chain, try to knock off the nose," Fields remembered, later adding, "I believe white people were talking to us about Jim Crow through that statue." Eventually, city leaders replaced the original Calhoun statue with a new one that rose several feet above the Charleston skyline on a pedestal far out of reach of the kind of vandalism Fields described. While no evidence confirms that the new monument towering over the Citadel Green was constructed in response to vandalism, black Charlestonians nonetheless took pride in the belief that they caused the change.[6]

Outside of safe spaces like private homes, churches, or a Masonic lodge, the fear of reprisal from local whites prohibited African American adults from making their feelings about monuments public in the Jim Crow South.[7] Even Mamie Garvin Fields did not disclose her opinions until several decades after segregation ended. Yet what she did say reveals much about what black citizens thought and felt about monuments dedicated to southern leaders who sought to keep them enslaved. In Charleston, they challenged the Calhoun statue's message by defacing it but did so cautiously, since they understood how tenuous their lives were. Openly defying the monument meant certain incarceration, if not worse. What's more, it is clear that Fields was not alone in her opinions. When she said that "blacks took that statue personally," she used the plural, because she understood that the larger black community shared her attitude about Confederate monuments. In fact, throughout the era of Jim Crow, African American newspapers, both in and out of the South, offer proof that such sentiments were widespread.

For example, African American Richmonders held similar views about the equestrian statue of Robert E. Lee in their hometown, which they expressed through the local black newspaper, the *Richmond Planet*. When the Lee monument was unveiled in May 1890, the paper reported that "Confederates from New York to Texas" who were in town for the unveiling demonstrated their continued commitment to Confederate values, behaving as if the South had not lost the Civil War. The display of "rebel flags," including one "mammoth Confederate flag" that covered the entire length of city hall, alongside the gathering of Confederate veterans giving a full-throated "rebel yell . . . told in no uncertain tones that they still clung to theories which were presumably to be buried for all eternity." While the paper's editor, John Mitchell Jr., did not begrudge the entirety of the ceremonies, acknowledging that "the South may revere the memory of its chieftains," he felt that the region "proceeds to go too far in every similar celebration." Doing so not only was a deterrent to progress, he lamented, but also "forge[d] heavier chains with which to be bound."[8]

Barely a week after the unveiling of the Lee monument, Mitchell sounded a different alarm. There was more than just a new statue at issue. In an editorial titled "What of Virginia," Mitchell warned readers that the rights blacks had won during Reconstruction were being rolled back. He printed the words of the Fifteenth Amendment, which guaranteed the right to vote regardless of "race, color, or previous condition of servitude," and pointed out that the amendment was now under attack, adding, "There must be a remedy."[9]

But there was no remedy in the 1890s South, as states across the region took steps to disfranchise black voters. And it was not a coincidence that the Lost Cause fed that movement as much as it did the building of Confederate monuments. John Mitchell knew it, as did editors of black newspapers elsewhere. Two weeks after the Lee monument was unveiled, Mitchell printed a sampling of editorials in a column called "The Voice of the Colored Press," which detailed African Americans' concerns about the meaning of the unveiling to their race. "The exhibitions of rebel flags on all holiday occasions in the South is not the only way the people of that section show that they have not accepted the results of war," a Detroit paper lamented, while a paper from Springfield, Illinois, wrote of the "shameful disregard for the flag of the Union and of higher respect for the flag of treason" during the unveiling of the Lee monument in Richmond. A Baltimore paper cautioned that the celebration of Lee and the Lost Cause served "as an opportunity to justify the rebellion of the southern people against the U.S. Government and to flaunt the Confederate flag in the faces of the loyal people of the nation" and deserved "serious reflection." Lee, after all, had "bound himself under oath to support and . . . extend the accursed institution of human slavery." From Louisville, an editor was far more pointed in his criticism of the festivities in Richmond. "They hold their lives by the mercy of the nation they attempted to destroy," he wrote, "and this rehabilitation of the infamous cause of the Confederacy is rank treason." As black southerners throughout the region knew, the rehabilitation of the Confederacy was accompanied by the rise of white supremacy in the 1890s, and monuments were demonstrations of that fact.[10]

Throughout the first half of the twentieth century, African Americans continued to express their contempt for Confederate symbols. The *Chicago Defender*, founded in 1905, quickly became a nationally respected black newspaper, and its pages were a lively space for both journalists and readers to voice their opinion on Confederate flags and monuments. Many of its columnists were migrants from the South, and the paper was read and shared throughout the region.

From the outset, the *Defender* published pieces that linked monuments to both slavery and treason, and writers were very clear about what should be done with them. A 1920 article about a recently discovered bill of sale for a thirteen-year-old enslaved girl in Tuscaloosa, Alabama, was intended as a lesson to "the younger generation." The buyer, who could neither read nor write, had signed the document with an "X," the *Defender* told readers, "signifying he was ignorant." Yet it was in the closing paragraph where the paper zeroed in on slavery's link to the Lost Cause. The story of the sale of a young black girl, the *Defender* argued, was "testimony enough to justify the statement that every Confederate monument standing under the Stars and Stripes should be torn down and ground into pebbles."[11]

The following year, a staff correspondent writing from Thomasville, Georgia, published an unsigned article under the headline "Tear the Spirit of the Confederacy from the South—Destroy All Flags, Records and Other Symbols of Ante-Bellum Days." Given the tenor of the piece, it is clear why the author remained anonymous, since revealing his identity (writers at this time in the *Defender's* history were male) would have put his life in danger. The article began as a response to protests against a statue of John Wilkes Booth in Alabama that had been placed there in 1906 but had received national attention, including in the northern press. This monument to the "murderer of the Emancipator" led the author to rail against Confederate iconography in southern communities and to present a searing critique of the Lost Cause. "In every Southern city, town or hamlet one sees relics of the Confederacy kept intact," he wrote. "Confederate flags fly triumphantly, monuments are erected to Lee, the victories of rebels are celebrated, museums gather obsolete weapons, libraries store the infamous records, white school children are studiously taught to believe in the righteousness of the lost cause," he complained, and all of it was done "to reproduce the spirit of ante-bellum days."[12]

The author's detailed description of Confederate culture in the South, much of it a result of the United Daughters of the Confederacy's efforts, is a vivid reminder of how widespread the Lost Cause was and how embedded it had become even in communities with a significant African American population. He recog-

nized a direct link between these symbols and the disfranchisement of his race. "Every Confederate flag in the South should be
sought out and burned," he wrote, adding that "it should be made
a misdemeanor to display one" and that parades that honored
rebels "should be made a crime." Sectionalism was the problem,
he argued, because it "propped up" Confederate traditions. And
he pointed the finger at public schools, churches, and newspapers
for the "incalculable wrong" they were doing to black southerners, especially in public schools, justly noting how the continued
instruction of Lost Cause ideals perpetuated racism among the
next generation of white southerners: "The Southern white child
goes to school to find an emblem of Jefferson Davis' South hung
beside Old Glory. He is taught that the old ideals are still right. . . .
The Southern white child is taught and led to believe that he is a
superior being; that the law which granted freedom and opportunity to our Race may be easily glossed over; that he does not have
to obey it."[13]

Roscoe Simmons, an editor of the *Chicago Defender* in the
1920s, published a popular column called "The Week" in which he
wrote about several news items of interest to readers. Confederate monuments were prime targets. Simmons, a native Mississippian, did not hold back in his estimation of the South and the Lost
Cause. Writing in 1923, he observed, "The Civil War is still being
fought. It will never be over as long as the memory of Lee, flower
of the South, lives." He made his sentiments known to leading
Republican politicians, he explained, telling one member of the
party that "the G. O. P. would be able to carry Dixie when every
Confederate monument is as sand under foot and the memory of
Lee and Jefferson Davis has passed from every record."[14]

Simmons's assessment of the Stone Mountain memorial in
progress just outside of Atlanta illustrated his frustration, and yet
he encouraged his readers to remain hopeful. He began his column on Stone Mountain, "Another monument for you. You will
be glad to read of it, think about it, saying to yourself, it never
rains unless it pours." Stone Mountain, of course, was intended
to be the largest Confederate memorial to inhabit the southern
landscape. Yet Simmons offered an uplifting message. "Whatever
may be written on the side of Stone Mountain will not disturb

the Emancipation Proclamation," he reminded readers. "What is NOT written will be more important to you . . . than what is written." Then, speaking as the personification of Liberty, he suggested what she might say to members of the race: "See the faces of those who struggled against you but indulge no regrets. Though I struggled for you and won, my picture is not there, but you will find it in the hearts of men. . . . Then you will clap your hands."[15]

The *Chicago Defender* regularly engaged its readers, asking them their thoughts about any number of topics that were of interest to the race in a column called "What Do You Say about It?" On September 10, 1932, the paper printed the answers to the question it posed the prior week. The question "Would you favor a federal law to abolish all patriotic monuments erected in the South to the memory of Confederate soldiers?" elicited several favorable responses. Spencer Hilt of Columbus, Georgia, wrote, "I am highly in favor of such a law," and pointed disapprovingly to the federal government for "[tolerating] the unpatriotic spirit of the South to the Stars and Stripes." Hilt added, "Rebels should not be honored, and any section of the country producing traitors should be ashamed of them." John Upcher, a reader from Omaha, Nebraska, was troubled by what monuments taught young white southerners. "Every time children of the men [Confederate veterans] look at the monuments it gives them a greater desire to . . . carry out the wishes of their forefathers," he worried, adding, "If those monuments weren't standing the white South wouldn't be so encouraged to practice hate and discrimination against our people." In short, he said, "They stand as emblems of hate and envy" and "shouldn't have been permitted" to be erected. A letter from Scott Boydston of Birmingham, Alabama, began by calling out the Lost Cause: "The dirtiest blot on the pages of American History was written by rebel statesmen of the South. Why honor them?" He suggested that Confederate monuments were the equivalent of one "to the memory of Benedict Arnold." He believed that the South held the nation back and concluded by writing, "Only fools would want to glorify men who fought in defense of human slavery."[16]

These letters offer insight into how African Americans from various places around the South saw the monuments in their communities on a daily basis. They also demonstrated the writers' keen understanding of American history and what patriotism meant to them. Further, they revealed the hold that the Lost Cause had on the region, so much that "the South has never admitted defeat," M. K. Quigley of Marietta, Georgia, wrote. Quigley expressed his belief that the North went too easy on the South at war's end. "Jeff Davis should have been shot at sunrise and his whole staff imprisoned for life," he said, and "to honor these skunks with monuments for the future generation to gaze upon is the rawest insult to the memory of noble men like Lincoln and Grant." Marshfield Gregg of Waynesboro, a fellow Georgian, agreed. "It is a blot on civilization that at this time and day we are faced with granites that depict men who attempted to perpetuate human slavery."[17]

The responses of African Americans to the *Defender*'s question offered stark evidence that Confederate monuments meant something far different to them from what white southerners claimed they symbolized. Confederate organizations, especially the UDC, were still busy building monuments when the paper queried its readers about a federal law banning such iconography. By the early 1930s, there were already several hundred markers and statues erected throughout the region. While black southerners covertly defiled Confederate monuments from the time they were unveiled, they did not publicly protest such symbols for fear of being attacked, indeed lynched, for such views, but they registered their contempt in the pages of the nation's leading African American newspapers.[18] And the contents of their letters reveal not simply the opinion of an individual writer; they suggest that entire communities of black southerners had concluded that Confederate monuments represented white supremacy and treason as well as honored white men who would have kept them enslaved. In this, they were in agreement with W. E. B. Du Bois, who wrote after a visit to the South that a better inscription to include on monuments to the Confederacy would be "Sacred to the memory of those who fought to Perpetuate Human Slavery."[19]

With the coming of the 1920s and 1930s, monument building slowed, and the Second World War brought it to a near halt. By then, the vast majority of monuments we know of today were already in place. Regardless, there were still ways to insinuate a memorial to the Confederacy, such as by naming places after heroes of the Lost Cause. And on December 7, 1940, one year to the day before the United States entered World War II, a soldiers' training camp in Tennessee was one of those places. Camp Peay, named for former governor Austin Peay, was singled out for a name change by Brigadier General T. A. Frazier, who urged the U.S. War Department to rename the camp after Confederate general Nathan Bedford Forrest. While noted for his military exploits, Forrest had been a slave trader and, more notoriously, was a founder and first Grand Wizard of the Ku Klux Klan. The effort to change the name caught the eye of Lucius Harper, a columnist for the *Chicago Defender*, as well as of Major General Samuel T. Lawton, who commanded the Thirty-Third Division of Illinois. Lawton expressed dismay that the camp would honor Forrest, who, he explained to Tennessee officials, was "distasteful to a large number of Illinois citizens." Harper, a Georgia native, was more pointed in his criticism. In his column "Dustin' Off the News," he began his critique of the name change, writing, "The South is a hard loser. It is forever re-fighting the Civil War." Continuing to honor soldiers who "shot bullet holes through the Stars and Stripes" reflected an inability on the part of the South to accept its defeat eighty-five years after the war ended. As Harper pointed out, "Almost every southern city has its main street bedecked with granite monuments to these traitors, and every Y.M.C.A. is more or less a Confederate museum." The suggestion that "one of the rankest, vilest, most brutal and ignorant slave traders be highly honored by having a U.S. soldiers' camp named after him" was too much for Harper. Nonetheless, the name changed occurred with the endorsement of the U.S. Army.[20]

Despite black resistance, the Lost Cause remained a strident part of white culture in the South through World War II, and as the renaming of the base in Tennessee demonstrates, it benefited from the complicity of national government entities. It continued unabated following the war but broadened to take on new messaging about states' rights in the face of racial change, as well as a "patriotic" defense against communism. In this context, monuments assumed new meanings.

■ ■ ■

The role of Confederate monuments in the South at midcentury must be understood in the context of the changes wrought by the Second World War. That war, as much as the Civil War, was a watershed moment in the region's history. It contributed to the South's economic modernization, urbanization, and demographic changes, not to mention shifts in politics and race relations. Southern Democrats may have supported Franklin Roosevelt's defense program as a way to create new business and industrial opportunities, as well as to open up the region to economic development in the early 1940s, but they were particularly concerned with policies they saw as tampering with the southern social order. As a result, they made alliances with conservative Republicans, even as they distanced themselves from the national Democratic Party. When their party, led by President Harry Truman, introduced a civil rights platform in 1948, they drew a line in the sand, which led to the Dixiecrat Revolt. The States' Rights Democratic Party, as it was formally known, was short-lived; however, southern congressmen continued to fight civil rights legislation tooth and nail.[21]

Demographically, the South became less rural during the war. African Americans, who made up most of the rural population of the South, accounted for nearly two-thirds of the out-migration of southerners who moved North and West and for nearly half of those who moved to southern cities.[22] Significantly, those blacks who remained in the South and moved to its urban centers began grassroots organizing for civil rights as soon as the war ended. These efforts were led by returning World War II veterans influenced by the Double V campaign started by the *Pittsburgh Courier* during the war. The double "victory" referred to a victory over fascism abroad and over white supremacy at home. Black veterans who took the campaign to heart included Medgar Evers, who became field secretary for the NAACP in Mississippi, and Harry Briggs, the plaintiff in a legal case against segregation in Clarendon County, South Carolina, that paved the way for the 1954 Supreme Court case *Brown v. Board of Education*, outlawing racial segregation in public schools. After fighting in a war to preserve democracy overseas, black veterans like Evers and Briggs were motivated to advocate for a more representative democracy at home in the United States.[23]

The battle for civil rights in the South was slow and measured at first, but in the aftermath of Emmett Till's murder, it picked up steam. By the early 1960s, young men and women of Till's generation drew attention to their cause through direct action. The sit-ins began in February 1960 in Greensboro, North Carolina, with students from North Carolina A&T University and spread rapidly across the South. In 1961, the Freedom Rides tested federal laws prohibiting segregation on interstate buses. Two years later, in 1963, the March on Washington brought a quarter of a million people to Washington, D.C., to make the case for equality. In 1964, the Civil Rights Act, signed by President Lyndon Johnson, outlawed discrimination based on race, color, religion, sex, or national origin. The Voting Rights Act of 1965 prohibited racial discrimination in voting. All of this was rapid change indeed for white southerners, and resistance came in many forms, including violence.

Significantly, white southerners revived the Lost Cause in the 1950s and 1960s in their fight against integration and civil rights. Southern legislatures passed laws to add the Confederate battle flag design into their state flags, and segregationists ranging from the Citizens Councils of America, also known as the "white collar Klan," to homegrown racists drew from Lost Cause narratives about states' rights, federal intervention, and even Reconstruction. The Ku Klux Klan, well known for its use of Confederate iconography, resurrected long-held beliefs about protecting white women and girls from black men, stoked fears of interracial marriage and the "mongrelization" of the white race, and used all of it to justify lynching.

Southern politicians also deployed Lost Cause rhetoric in defense of segregation, including, most famously, Alabama governor George Wallace. While his 1963 inauguration speech is remembered for the line "segregation now, segregation tomorrow, segregation forever," it began with language that might have been heard during a monument unveiling speech decades earlier. Standing on the steps of the Alabama State Capitol "where Jefferson Davis once stood," Wallace asserted how "appropriate" it was that he spoke "from this Cradle of the Confederacy, this very Heart of the Great

Anglo-Saxon Southland." He railed against federal intrusion into states' rights over issues of integration and civil rights, calling it "the tyranny that clanks its chains upon the South." In essence, Wallace drew from the Confederate tradition in issuing his call to arms against integration because it was language familiar to most white Alabamians who were raised on its tenets.[24]

During the Civil War centennial, between 1961 and 1965, the Lost Cause was on full display across the South. While Congress authorized $100,000 per year for centennial commemorations, individual states funded commemorative activities at even higher amounts. In Mississippi, where the battle for civil rights was most intense, the state legislature appropriated $200,000 for the first two years of the centennial alone. Karl Betts, the first executive director of the Civil War Centennial Commission, testified before a House Appropriations subcommittee to explain how the money was being used, including for Civil War reenactments. According to Betts, "Local organizations were so eager to start shooting that it was almost impossible to restrain them." He noted that the "urge to stage battles," especially in the South, "has reached such proportions . . . they are commemorating their defeats as well as their victories."[25]

White southerners had long memorialized the region's defeat and transformed their vanquished Confederate ancestors into heroes. The revival of Confederate culture and its symbols at midcentury, therefore, was not simply about commemorating heritage. Rather, it served the additional purpose of drawing white southerners together to rebel against the Second Reconstruction —civil rights. It was clear that the UDC's call to create "living monuments" to the Confederacy in the early twentieth century and members' investment in educating children about the Lost Cause had born fruit. Those children, now adults, were doing exactly as the Daughters had hoped they would. They became stalwart defenders of states' rights and honored their Confederate ancestors by fighting to preserve racial segregation.

Physical statues had their place, too, although dedications moved forward at a slower pace than during the early twentieth century's fever pitch. Between 1950 and 1969, an estimated thirty-four new Confederate monuments were dedicated.[26] During these same years, the generation of southerners who grew up on the Lost Cause narrative created new types of memorials to their forebears. Of the 109 schools named for Confederate heroes, for example, 39 were named during this period. The hundreds of monuments that were built generations earlier still served a purpose as sites of commemoration but also for rallying segregationists. This new generation imbued them with new meaning. Ultimately, southern states used the Civil War centennial to reaffirm the Confederate tradition during the very years that the civil rights movement entered its most significant phase.

■ ■ ■

When the 1950s began, the United States was fighting a war in Korea, while on the home front television shows like *Amos 'n' Andy*, which revived the characters of the popular radio show of the same name, and *Beulah*, which starred Hattie McDaniel, who had won an Oscar for her portrayal of Mammy in *Gone with the Wind*, still portrayed African American men as buffoons and black women as maids. Both shows ended their runs in 1953, due in large part to the backlash of the NAACP and, in the case of *Amos 'n' Andy*, a boycott of the show's sponsor, Blatz Brewing Company. For African Americans, the battle for equality also included a battle against cultural stereotypes.[27]

On the other hand, the 1950s was a successful decade for the United Daughters of the Confederacy, in terms of both meeting fundraising goals for pet projects and ramping up its education efforts through scholarships and its auxiliary, the Children of the Confederacy. In the context of concerns over states' rights across the South and fears of communism nationally, the UDC settled into a new role as a patriotic organization whose work with children, especially, was encouraged and welcomed by white male leaders in the region. In this way, the Daughters continued the work of their foremothers to create a new generation of "living

(opposite) Confederate monuments were long used as instructional tools for white schoolchildren. The lessons were still being taught during the civil rights movement, as this photograph in front of the Lee monument in Richmond, Virginia, in 1951, illustrates. (Courtesy of the Richmond Times-Dispatch Collection, The Valentine)

monuments" among white children growing up in an atmosphere of violent opposition to integration.

Physical monuments and memorials were still part and parcel of the UDC's objectives, however, and in 1949 members voted to build a headquarters for the organization billed as a "Memorial to the Women of the Confederacy," the most expensive project the group had engaged in since Stone Mountain. Several cities made their bid for the headquarters, including Jackson, Mississippi; Montgomery, Alabama; and Charleston, South Carolina. In the end, the UDC chose Richmond, Virginia. According to a spokeswoman, the organization made its selection not only because Richmond had once served as the capital of the Confederacy but also because the State of Virginia had "offered to provide land and financial assistance in building the headquarters." The land, as it turned out, was the former site of Virginia's Confederate soldiers' home, located between the Battle Abbey (now the Virginia Museum of History and Culture) and the Virginia Museum of Fine Arts. In some ways, the women were putting the cart before the horse, since getting the land required that the state, which had title to the property, would transfer it to the UDC. But the Daughters were confident, telling members that "if the committee were not definitely sure that this transfer of title was an easy matter, we would not recommend this site to you."[28]

Nonetheless, the UDC, during the meeting of the general organization in 1950, hesitated to proceed with the building, despite having blueprints in hand. The price tag of $250,000 gave some members pause, such that the budget was cut by half and the project was tabled until 1951. And yet, during the same convention, the UDC voted overwhelmingly to spend $45,000 on a memorial stained glass window in honor of Robert E. Lee to be placed in the Washington National Cathedral.[29] Over the next few years, the organization continued fundraising for the new headquarters and encouraged competition among state divisions. In Richmond, members revived the "Confederate Ball," whose proceeds were meant for the building fund, but the event often operated in the red. Even though the *Times-Dispatch* called the January 1954 ball a "financial failure," Mrs. James T. Avery, president-general of the Stonewall Jackson Chapter of the UDC, still considered it a "magnificent success." While it may have been a social success, Avery blamed the poor receipts on the fact that "there were some 600 gate crashers."[30]

Despite the financial losses of the Confederate Ball, the very next month the UDC headquarters committee announced it had approved new blueprints for a headquarters building, whose budget now stood at $300,000. How had the women gone from slashing the budget by half for the building in 1950 to more than doubling it only a few years later? While it is not exactly clear how, the Daughters may have financially benefited from the fact that the civil rights movement was gaining ground and members were rallying around the southern cause of the 1950s: segregation. The UDC's support for that cause, therefore, likely boosted fundraising for the headquarters.

Additionally, by 1954 the group finally had title to the land in Richmond and expected to break ground on the building the following year. Mrs. L. B. Newell of Charlotte, North Carolina, spokeswoman for the committee, announced that the UDC had raised $175,000 toward construction. She and her fellow committee members were in Richmond to share this news and to meet with Governor Thomas Stanley. Their meeting with the governor was intentional, though they claimed it was a "purely social call." They also sought to "confer" with state senator Garland Gray.[31]

The Daughters' meetings with leading southern politicians had long been a common tactic to garner political and financial support for their projects, especially monuments and memorials. During the early Jim Crow period, women who did not have the right to vote still met with their state legislators and local boards of commissioners. Very often they were related by blood or marriage to those men, so their requests were frequently successful. By the 1950s, the UDC still had the power to call for meetings with men of influence in the region. Together, they shared the common goal of maintaining racial segregation, and in Virginia, two of the main leaders of massive resistance to desegregation were none other than Governor Stanley and Senator Gray. After the *Brown* decision, the governor appointed the senator to head the newly formed Virginia Public Education Commission to recommend a legislative response. The Gray Commission, as it became known, unsurprisingly issued a report defending racial segregation in public schools. Among one of its recommendations was that the state amend its constitution to allow for an educational voucher program for parents who did not want to send their children to integrated schools. These were southern men the UDC could count on.[32]

When the Daughters' headquarters building officially opened in November 1957, final costs had risen to $375,000. State divisions of the UDC financed most of it, but the General Assembly of Virginia was true to its word, providing the organization a $10,000 appropriation. The building contained a library for records of Confederate soldiers, offices for UDC managers, and a central memorial hall. Two large bronze doors, cast in New Jersey for a sum of $25,000, were a gift of the Children of the Confederacy, the UDC's auxiliary.[33]

The Daughters had long thought it was important to involve children in the work of their organization. During the early twentieth century, children were taken to visit Confederate veterans at their state's soldiers' home, and the UDC involved children in raising money to build monuments. At local unveiling ceremonies, a child would be chosen to pull the cord that unveiled the monument, a symbolic act showing that a direct connection existed between the Confederate past and future generations of white southerners. The group's engagement with children continued in the 1950s, as the Daughters sought to build up the Children of the Confederacy as well as groom southern youth to question federal intervention into states' rights.

Education had always been a central UDC objective, and it took on added emphasis in the 1950s. At the general organization's convention in Richmond in 1957, not only did members celebrate the opening of the new headquarters; they also gave special awards to state divisions that had done outstanding work in education, singling out UDC members in North Carolina and Virginia for "best work in educational films." A special feature of the convention was a speech given by seventeen-year-old John Chappell of Newberry, South Carolina. Chappell, the president-general of the Children of the Confederacy, demonstrated that he had learned the tenets of the Lost Cause well. The *Daily Press* of Newport News, Virginia, reported that the teen expressed concern that "today's writers and historians are trying to distort history." There were other culprits, too. "Modern radicals and liberals are trying to warp the minds of Southern young people to the point where they will want to hide their ancestors in a closet," he warned. Taking a page from the Daughters, he advised that the best defense against such "revisionism" was to have "more true Southern historians to write and publish books, and after they are published, try to get state and local authorities to adopt them as standard textbooks."[34]

The focus of Confederate heritage organizations in the 1950s reflected the concerns of white southerners more broadly, whether history, states' rights, or fears of communism. At the root of these issues, of course, was their hostility toward changes in race relations. During the November 1954 general convention of the UDC, President-General Mrs. Belmont Dennis of Covington, Georgia, called on delegates to denounce communism, place "God first in every life," and focus on "stamp[ing] out the Red threat."[35] White conservatives, including UDC members, faulted communism for having infiltrated the civil rights movement and for disrupting race relations and the system of segregation. In this, Confederate organizations were not unlike the region's Citizens' Councils, whose motto, "States' rights and racial integrity," was widely shared.[36] In fact, the UDC regularly invited to its meetings speakers who repurposed the Confederate past for modern-day battles. In Chattanooga, Tennessee, the local newspaper editor addressed the 1956 state convention of the UDC, telling members that the push for desegregation was an "attack on states' rights" and a "threat to freedom." One year earlier, James Price, a local attorney in Greenville, South Carolina, gave a speech to the local UDC chapter titled "States Rights." He urged members to "keep alive the UDC by passing on the organization's ideals and principles to their children" and closed by reading the words on the local Confederate monument in Springwood Cemetery:

> Success is not the test
> The world shall yet decide
> In truth's clear far off light
> That the soldiers

Who wore the gray and died
With Lee, were right.[37]

As the decade came to a close, support for the Civil War centennial became part of the ongoing defense of states' rights in
the South. A national grassroots campaign to commemorate the
American Civil War emerged in the early 1950s, and in 1958 it finally yielded results. That year Congress approved the creation of
the U.S. Civil War Centennial Commission (CWCC) along with
an appropriation of $100,000 to help plan events, and over the
next few years several states set up their own centennial commissions in anticipation of the four-year commemoration. Across
the South, and especially in the Deep South, southern states reeling from negative press over their resistance to integration saw
the centennial as opportunity to showcase their role in shaping
American history and to demonstrate national unity. But patriotic rhetoric to the contrary, the region remained committed
to the Lost Cause version of the Civil War past and ultimately
participated in the centennial as a means of combating the civil
rights movement.[38]

Southern state centennial commissions from Virginia to Mississippi were led by segregationists and members of Confederate
organizations. In both Alabama and Mississippi, the state commissions were filled with members of the UDC and the Sons of
Confederate Veterans, while Virginia congressman and former
governor William M. Tuck, a staunch segregationist, both headed
the Virginia Centennial Commission and served as a prominent
member of the national CWCC. When the commemoration was
inaugurated in Richmond, Tuck's message was restrained. "We are
not re-fighting the Civil War—we are restudying it," he said. Yet
across the state, the centennial took on the tone of the Lost Cause
with the rededication of the Confederate monument in Alexan-
dria; ceremonies marking the arrival of the Confederate government from Montgomery, Alabama; commemoration of the place
where the first Confederate soldier was killed; and the opening
of a special exhibit on Robert E. Lee at his birthplace, Stratford.[39]

State funding for centennial activities was critical and varied by
state. In Virginia, which expected to enjoy an influx of tourist dol-

lars during the four-year celebration, the legislature appropriated $1.75 million, much of which went to building a visitors' center in Richmond. Tennessee's and Georgia's appropriation of $10,000 and $25,000, respectively, paled by comparison. The Mississippi Commission on the War between the States, as it was named, provided a more generous allocation of $200,000 for the centennial. The Mississippi Commission was, as historian Alyssa Warrick has noted, "unapologetically pro-Confederate" and often used commemorative activities to criticize communism and liberalism and drive home a defiant message of preserving states' rights in the cause of segregation.[40]

The South's commitment to Lost Cause principles, its dedication and rededication of Confederate monuments, and its intractability on the race question led to significant differences with the CWCC, whose advisory board was chaired by historian Allan Nevins. In its final report to Congress in 1966, the commission acknowledged that "friction over racial issues" in the South had led to resentment over the CWCC's insistence on including African Americans in the commemoration. The report, likely written by Nevins, explained that "it was impossible to disassociate the racial issue from the Civil War," and the commission refused to compromise on this point. "Not only had emancipation been one of the great turning points of the war," but "the 13th, 14th, and 15th amendments had grown out of the war," the report noted, adding, "The Negro had every right to share in the Centennial on equal terms with the white man."[41]

Nonetheless, the commemoration of the Civil War drew sharp criticism from the black community, particularly from Lawrence Reddick, an African American historian who earned his Ph.D. from the University of Chicago. Reddick was teaching at Alabama State University when he attended the first mass meeting concerning the Montgomery bus boycott; he eventually became friends with Martin Luther King Jr. and authored the book *Crusader without Violence*, the first biography of King. As a southerner and a historian, he had a clear understanding of how the white South used the Lost Cause as a cudgel against racial progress. In a speech given before 2,000 members of the New York Teachers Union in May 1961, Reddick blasted the centennial for "perpetuating the

'Confederacy myth,'" stating that it represented both a "psychological and political resistance" to black civil rights.[42]

The Civil War centennial, in many ways, served as a microcosm of continued regional differences, not simply over Civil War memory but also on the issue of race, as Reddick's speech conveyed. While the federally appointed CWCC sought to be racially inclusive, white leaders of state commissions across the South perpetuated the Lost Cause narrative of states' rights and its attendant white supremacy. On the very day that Virginia inaugurated its centennial celebration in April 1961, for example, the St. Helena Parish school board in Greensburg, Louisiana, voted to close its public schools rather than integrate. State law gave it that right, but not federal law. It was all a show for segregation, not unlike many of the centennial celebrations across the South.[43]

■ ■ ■

Midcentury Confederate culture may not have produced as many monuments as the bumper years of the early 1900s, but these years saw white southerners embrace the hundreds of statues already in their midst, fueled by the UDC's education program to regard them as sacred symbols of a historical legacy. Yes, there were new monuments, like the Alabama Memorial at Vicksburg National Military Park, for which the Alabama State Legislature allocated $150,000 in 1950. Yes, there were rededications, like that of the North Carolina Monument at Gettysburg Military Park during the Civil War centennial. Yet it was the reanimation of existing monuments that stand out during the 1950s and 1960s, as white southerners embraced Confederate culture and its meaning in the midst of racial upheaval.[44]

Traditionally, Confederate monuments served as a gathering place on Confederate Memorial Day, the timing of which varied by state. These annual ceremonies nearly always involved children, and this remained true at midcentury. In April 1955, for example, approximately 300 white students from the local public schools of Selma, Alabama, observed memorial day ceremonies during their assembly period. Sixth graders at one school recited poems such as "Men in Gray" and sang "Dixie," a seventh-grade girl read her UDC contest-winning essay "Alabama Women of the Sixties," and one school displayed the battle flag alongside portraits of Jefferson

Davis and Robert E. Lee. UDC members along with parents and children gathered for ceremonies around the local Confederate monument, too, where a Boy Scout played reveille on his bugle and students from a local elementary school placed flowers at the statue's base.[45]

Speeches had always been integral to Confederate Memorial Day activities, often given at the site of a monument, but in the 1950s they served as opportunities to criticize integration. In 1957, ceremonies in Vicksburg, Mississippi, included an address by the state's attorney general, Joseph Patterson. More than 200 people gathered to honor southern soldiers who had died during the siege of Vicksburg, and Patterson believed that the cause for which those men perished was again "under attack with greater force" than at any other time since the Civil War. "The Southland, especially our beloved state of Mississippi," he exclaimed, "is the target of a vicious propaganda campaign of half-truth and out-right misrepresentation." He expressed fury at the U.S. Supreme Court, which he asserted had assisted "sinister forces" whose aim was to destroy states' rights. Last, Patterson issued a call to arms to resist the move to "centralize all the governmental power in the federal government" as part and parcel of preserving the legacy of Confederate soldiers. Vicksburg's Confederate Memorial Day ceremonies had been dormant for over twenty years but were now, in 1957, revived in response to battles over integration. Certainly, the speaker chosen by the UDC suggests this was the case.[46]

That same year, "several thousand" people attended a birthday celebration of Jefferson Davis in Fairview, Kentucky, where the Confederate president was born in 1808. There, citizens of the state had dedicated a 351-foot-tall obelisk to Davis in 1924 at a cost of $200,000, but in 1957 a new generation of sympathizers gathered on the grounds around the monument to picnic, pay tribute, and partake in a celebration of the Confederacy. The *Louisville Courier-Journal* described the park as nearly covered in "the red and gray of the Confederate Army." Concession stands selling "Confederate Army flags, hats, and caps and other reminders of the Confederacy" did a swift business throughout the daylong celebration. A sixteen-year-old girl from Hopkinsville was crowned

"Miss Confederate," while one couple took their wedding vows on the monument's steps. The bride, a public schoolteacher, married a pre-law student from Western Kentucky State College (now University), who wore a Confederate army uniform. When a U.S. Army private waved a battle flag and shouted, "The South has risen again!," an old man resting next to the monument corrected him. "You're wrong son," he said; "the South never fell."[47]

Certainly, for black southerners, the living and breathing Confederacy, with all of its related symbols, made it feel as though Dixie never fell. Evidence of it was everywhere, especially in the Deep South, where civil rights struggles were toughest and white southerners continued to celebrate the Old South and the Confederacy. In Jackson, Mississippi, for example, the Kappa Alpha fraternity staged an Old South celebration in 1958 where young men dressed in Confederate uniforms and marched from the lawn of the Governor's Mansion to the grounds of the Old Capitol. The fraternity was joined by "a handful of refugees from Little Rock," a clear reference to segregationist battles in Arkansas, and upon their arrival at the capitol grounds they circled the Confederate monument and held a mock secession convention. There the group's "general" read aloud articles of secession that the Kappa Alphas invented for the occasion, each one "punctuated by the rebel yell." In addition to declaring the "emancipation of Southern Gentlemen," the "general" shouted, "We have been subjected to Yankee rule long enough," adding, "We do not intend to submit without a struggle."[48]

Politicians willingly participated in such festivities, too. While the streets of Jackson were lined with women dressed in hoop skirts and male students marched to declare their rejection of all things northern, Hinds County chancery judge Stokes Robertson Jr. and state senator Mitchell Robinson joined the parade in their car as self-proclaimed "retired generals" of the fraternity. The very next month, Robertson presided over Clennon King's "lunacy hearing" for trying to integrate the University of Mississippi. King sought to enroll in a graduate program in American history at Ole Miss but was rebuffed by administrators. When he refused to leave the registrar's office, he was arrested and taken to jail for disturbing the peace and resisting arrest, but his hearing rested on his mental stability. Judge Robertson ruled that King must go to the Mississippi State Insane Asylum, thus prohibiting integration at the state's flagship university. The judge's participation in a Confederate parade and his decision in the King case were connected by white supremacy.[49]

As the Old South festivities in Jackson show, Confederate monuments served the cause of segregation. While a mock secession speech may have appeared benign to white observers, such activities contained serious messages aimed at integration. Moreover, when white southerners claimed public spaces for celebrations of the Confederacy, including city streets and capitol grounds, it sent a message to black citizens that those same spaces not only were unwelcoming but stood for preserving the racial status quo.

Around the same time that young white southerners in Mississippi "seceded" from the North, a very different group took aim at members of the Texas state legislature who were filibustering against a segregation bill. These pro-segregationists, while not official lobbyists, came to the state capitol from Houston, Beaumont, and towns in East Texas. They announced their intention to hold a "giant" rally around the Confederate monument located on capitol grounds. Despite their attempt to make a symbolic stand at the Confederate monument, however, the "rally" drew few people and was rained out. Regardless, the significance was that they chose a symbol of white supremacy to help stake their claim against federally ordered integration.[50]

Texas was not Mississippi, but the legislature still had a strong segregationist contingent, and the House had passed several bills intended to stave off integration. What drew the pro-segregationists to Austin, however, was the filibuster against a segregation bill that had made its way to the state senate and encouraged local school districts to resist the federal order to integrate black and white children in Texas public schools. Henry Gonzalez, a Mexican American senator from San Antonio, stood on the senate floor for more than thirty-five hours railing against the bill. His fellow senator Abraham Kazan Jr., a Lebanese American representing the border town of Laredo, aided him by asking questions that allowed Gonzalez to rest his voice. The *Lubbock Morning Avalanche* reported that the two senators "trying to talk a segregation bill to death" faced the "prospect of defeat," but this did not dissuade either man.[51]

As the session went on into the night, a mixed-race crowd of more than 300 people were asked to leave the Senate chamber for cheering Gonzalez on. While on the floor, the senator also presented Kazan's amendment, whose intended effect was to kill the bill. This bill and Kazan's amendment were personal for both men. Kazan told reporters that his wife received a phone call in which he was referred to as a "n****r lover." Gonzalez, on the other hand, represented a district that was largely Hispanic and where integration already existed for Mexican American children. He feared that if the bill passed, it would lead to the resegregation of Hispanic students. "Is Texas liberty only the liberty of Anglo Saxons?" he asked. His efforts were for naught, and as soon as the filibuster ended, the legislation swiftly passed. Despite a temporary loss, legal segregation ended in the 1960s, although southern whites found other ways to prevent black and white children from attending school together. As the civil rights movement entered its most significant and violent phase in the early 1960s, segregation in higher education also came under scrutiny, and nowhere was it more violent than at the University of Mississippi. Unsurprisingly, the school's Confederate monument was central to events.[52]

■ ■ ■

James Meredith, a twenty-nine-year-old Air Force veteran and native Mississippian, had tried for eighteen months to enroll at the University of Mississippi following a court decision in his favor. Each time, he was turned away, but in the fall of 1962, he had the full force of the federal government behind him. This set up a tense standoff between Governor Ross Barnett, who repeatedly defied the court order allowing Meredith to register, and the young Kennedy administration, determined to enforce that order. Tensions finally came to a head in late September when President Kennedy federalized the Mississippi National Guard, mobilized the army and U.S. Marshals, and "ordered Mississippi to cease all obstruction to justice," while Governor Barnett took to the radio to proclaim, "We will never surrender."[53]

In what the *Chicago Defender* described as "the greatest threat to federal authority since the Civil War," Mississippi's governor

and state forces, as well as rogue students and white supremacists from nearby southern states, vowed to face off against federal
forces and to defy the president's executive order. Meredith was
escorted to campus on Sunday, September 30, and moved into
Baxter dormitory, while U.S. Marshals lined up in front of the Lyceum, Ole Miss's administration building.[54]

Just east of the Lyceum is the Circle, a parklike green space
at the entrance of the university, where people gathered out of
curiosity earlier in the day. But as day turned to night, the crowds
grew restless and swiftly turned into a riotous mob. Initially, they
tossed lit cigarettes and pebbles at the U.S. Marshals, but later they
turned to bricks, bottles, and even gunshot. State troopers, all of
whom were native white Mississippians, did nothing to preserve
the peace or protect the marshals and in some cases encouraged
the protesters, who taunted the federal officers with racial slurs.
Journalists assembled to document the event were also targeted.
One of them, Frenchman Paul Guihard, became the first casualty,
dying after being shot in the back. And there inside the Circle
stood the Confederate monument, a visible reminder of the
school's connection to white supremacy.

The twenty-nine-foot monument to Confederate soldiers, dedicated in 1906 by the local chapter of the Mississippi Division of
the United Daughters of the Confederacy, acted as a site of gathering during the Ole Miss Riot of 1962. While a 2016 report from
university historians claim that "there is no direct evidence that
rioters specifically rallied at the monument," it is clear from media
accounts that the Confederate statue played a key role in events,
particularly given its central location and the ways in which it was
used: first as a place of retreat from the tear gas used by U.S. Marshals, and second as the place where retired general Edwin Walker
stood to incite protesters to continue their fight.[55]

General Walker was a controversial figure but popular with
conservatives and white supremacists. He had commanded U.S.
forces at Little Rock, Arkansas, who were there to enforce integration of public schools, but in 1961 Secretary of Defense Robert
McNamara relieved him of his duties in Germany for "his rabidly
right-wing indoctrination of U.S. troops."[56] Walker then took the
step of retiring to his home in Dallas, Texas, rather than be si-

lenced by the military. After returning stateside, Walker went to Mississippi, where he gave a rousing speech defending state sovereignty and decrying communism. As tensions increased in Mississippi, he offered his "assistance" to Governor Barnett. He also took to the radio airwaves to call on fellow white conservatives to go to the university to defend the state from federal intrusion. Then on Saturday, September 29, the uninvited Walker drove to Oxford in anticipation of becoming involved in the showdown at Ole Miss. He offered his services to the local sheriff, who declined, but on the following day he made his way to campus to encourage the crowd of young white men, which included Ku Klux Klansmen, members of white Citizens' Councils, and students.[57]

The general entered the campus around 7:30 p.m. and chatted with students. A couple of hours later, as the mob grew more violent, the Texan strode over to the Confederate monument and climbed the steps of its base to speak to the crowd. Wearing a dark suit, white shirt, and his trademark Stetson hat, Walker spoke to those who had fallen back after a volley of tear gas was unleashed by U.S. Marshals. He told them to stand firm in support of their governor, promised there were reinforcements on the way, and proclaimed that if any blood was shed, it would be "on the hands of the Federal Government." The Reverend Duncan Gray, an Episcopal minister, also climbed onto the monument's pedestal, but he called for an end to violence. He was grabbed and roughed up before an officer led him to safety. Walker continued to fire up the mob. "Protest! Protest! Keep it up!" he shouted. Claude Sitton, a *New York Times* reporter, noted that "one of the mob's charges on the Lyceum . . . followed a harangue by [Walker] from the pedestal of the Confederate monument." When he stepped down, he began walking toward the Lyceum, 100 followers in tow. "Sic 'em John Birch," a student shouted.[58]

The following day, James Meredith enrolled at the University of Mississippi. Two people were dead and several others were injured, including U.S. Marshals. Al Kuettner, a UPI reporter, wrote, "It would be charitable to call what happened on the University of Mississippi campus a riot. It was more accurately a war—a pitched battle with knives, bullets, guns and tear gas." In Oxford, he saw how ingrained segregation was in the state and how even the idea of integration "pitted Americans against Americans in conflict unseen in the southland since the Civil War." And all of it was to prevent a young Air Force sergeant, with nine years of military service, the opportunity of an education in the state where he was born.[59]

In his book *Three Years in Mississippi*, published in 1966, Meredith mused about his graduation at Ole Miss on August 18, 1963, which involved students walking in a procession to the area known as the Grove, where commencement exercises are still held to this day. As they passed through the Lyceum, Meredith "took special notice of the bullet holes still there" from when he first arrived on campus, noting, "I had looked at those bullet holes many times." Upon leaving the Lyceum, he remembered, "We marched past the statue of the Confederate soldier, the symbol of the blood that had been shed one hundred years ago in defense of the system of 'White Supremacy,'" adding, "It was at the foot of this statue that General Walker had spoken to the crowd on the night of the revolt of the state of Mississippi."[60]

Meredith understood that the connection between the Confederate statue, the riot, and General Walker's speech from its steps represented a commitment to the racial status quo, and his observation offers us additional insight into the role of Confederate monuments at midcentury. The monuments built by the UDC in the early twentieth century were intentional symbols. They continued to "speak" to both white and black southerners decades later. White southerners understood these monuments as symbols of defiance—against racial inclusion, federal intrusion, and challenges to the southern way of life. African Americans understood that the hundreds of Confederate monuments spread throughout the southern landscape in places of prominence, whether in town squares, on courthouse lawns, or on university campuses, stood as symbols of racial inequality. Even after the Civil War centennial ended and hard-won civil rights legislation passed, monuments remained firmly in place. Although these symbols of the Lost Cause appeared dormant on the southern landscape, over the next several decades they continued to send out messages of defiance to white southerners still invested in the Confederate tradition and of injustice to black southerners and their supporters.

And as racial tensions have risen in southern culture, both sides have taken some of their cues from the lessons that Confederate monuments offer.

CODA

In 2006, the University of Mississippi unveiled a statue of James Meredith on its campus, intended to be a symbol of racial reconciliation at a university whose history was long tied to Confederate symbols of all kinds—flags, a monument, a rebel mascot, and a campus thoroughfare called "Confederate Drive." Meredith, though, was not given time to speak at the ceremony, and he later registered his distaste for the statue in his 2012 autobiography, calling on the university to destroy it. He wrote it was a "hideous presentation" that "makes no mention of my war against white supremacy." He despised the fact that the sculpture of him striding across campus had become "a soothing image on the civil rights tour of the South, a public relations tool for the powers that be at Ole Miss, and a feel-good icon of brotherly love and racial reconciliation."[61]

Two years after the publication of his memoir, the statue of Meredith was vandalized by students from the Sigma Phi Epsilon fraternity at Ole Miss. On the evening of February 15, 2014, Graeme Phillip Harris and Austin Reed Edenfield, both from Georgia, placed a noose around the head of the Meredith statue and draped it with one of the old Georgia state flags that incorporated the image of the Confederate battle flag. According to prosecutors, Harris devised the plan after an evening of drinking with Edenfield. They noted that Harris often made clear his dislike of black people, knowing full well that vandalizing the statue would, at the very least, upset the campus community. "It's James Meredith," he told Edenfield. "People will go crazy." The following day, the two returned to watch events unfold, and Harris raised his fist and shouted, "White power!" It was caught on video and led to the arrest and prosecution of both men.[62]

James Meredith did not change his mind about his own statue, calling it a "supplicant" to the system of white supremacy, not unlike the Confederate monument that then stood 100 yards away, because neither addressed the fundamental problem of racism that still exists, not only in Mississippi but across America. The "lynching" of the Meredith statue in Oxford in 2014 proved that the messages of Confederate culture continued to inspire new generations.[63]

4

MONUMENTS AND THE BATTLE FOR FIRST-CLASS CITIZENSHIP

In the aftermath of the passage of the Voting Rights Act, black southerners boldly called out and protested the message of white supremacy that Confederate monuments represented. They expressed contempt for all Confederate symbols, especially the Confederate battle flag, that were used to menace those pushing for racial justice. And their disdain for monuments became more pronounced after 1965.

■ ■ ■

Prior to World War II, African American critiques of monuments had been vociferous, but after the war, the Confederate battle flag proved more noxious. African American journalists frequently commented on the insidiousness of "rebel flags." Hung in public spaces, draped from balconies for parades, or used by segregationists to taunt black southerners as they sought to integrate schools or register to vote, Confederate flags were easily obtainable and a highly mobile tool of intimidation. They also proved to be politically malleable—during the 1960 presidential race, for example, Richard Nixon's campaign was often "met by large enthusiastic crowds waving Confederate flags."[1]

As far north as New York, Confederate flags were being deployed as instruments of intimidation, which caused alarm even among northern moderates. In 1963, Amos Basel, a candidate for councilman-at-large in Manhattan, called for a municipal law to ban "the sale, distribution or display of the Confederate flag." His desire for the ordinance came in the aftermath of a "hoodlum demonstration" against the Congress of Racial Equality in the Bronx. Basel, who was no civil rights activist, still worried about the "wide use of this symbol of bigotry and slavery," which he equated with the Nazi flag. Southerners certainly understood the flag's ability to cause offense. After Harlem assemblyman Lloyd Dickens sponsored legislation against the display of the battle flag in New York, he received numerous letters and postcards from the South with photos of the Confederate flag. One person sent the New Yorker's wife a bumper sticker of the flag with a note that read, "This attractive sticker is for Mr. Dickens' auto." Within a few decades, Confederate flags would become an unremarkable sight in upstate New York, on Staten Island, or in certain neighborhoods in the city, but in the 1960s it was truly regarded as offensive. Of course, it was in the South, especially the Deep South, where the flag was used to instill fear.[2]

Meanwhile, Confederate monuments remained ever present in the ongoing battle for racial justice. While such statues were part and parcel of southern heritage for some white southerners, the longer history of these symbols and their meaning for black southerners were not far from the minds of civil rights activists. Confederate monuments stood above them as they entered the courthouses to register to vote or marched into town along certain thoroughfares, and even more were being erected. After the passage of both the Civil Rights Act of 1964 and the Voting Rights Act of 1965, the long history of disdain for these symbols came bubbling to the surface. The ways in which black southerners interacted with Confederate monuments became notably more assertive. Once elected to office in local government, some took formal action to oppose them. What had long been said in black newspapers or in the company of friends and family was now being said out loud and accompanied by the reclamation of the public spaces where monuments stood.

■ ■ ■

As the civil rights movement won notable legislative victories, black southerners were increasingly insistent in claiming the right not only to vote but also to occupy community space that, under the gaze of Confederate statues, had been barred to them. The push to register African American voters, especially in states like Mississippi where white resistance remained fierce, took on added importance, as did confrontations with monuments. This confluence of events was evident in 1966 when James Meredith—both a military veteran and a veteran in the battle against white supremacy, having integrated the University of Mississippi a few years before—decided on his own to lead a march from Memphis, Tennessee, through the heart of the Mississippi Delta, where large swaths of African Americans were still not registered to vote.[3]

Some white Mississippians, still angry that he had integrated the state's flagship university, were prepared to rid the state of Meredith even if it meant killing him. He did not hesitate. Mississippi was his home, too, and black Mississippians were family. He sought to use the march not only to register voters but to help buoy people who were afraid to vote, which is why he called the journey between Memphis and Jackson, Mississippi, a "March Against Fear."[4] His trip, however, was cut short by a gunman, not far outside of Hernando, who emerged with a shotgun from the brush that lined the highway. He fired two shots, knocking Meredith to the ground, and then shot him a third time at close range before walking away. The police accompanying the marchers did nothing to stop him.[5]

An ambulance whisked Meredith to a hospital in Memphis, where doctors pronounced him to be in satisfactory condition— but this did not stop the press from announcing that he had died, sending shock waves throughout the United States. Once it was clear that Meredith did indeed survive, leaders from all the major civil rights organizations, north and south, saw an opportunity to galvanize people for the ongoing fight for equality. Both old guard and new guard civil rights leaders vowed to continue what he had begun. Eventually, Stokely Carmichael, Floyd McKissick, and Martin Luther King Jr.—the leaders of the Student Nonviolent Coordinating Committee (SNCC), the Congress of Racial Equality (CORE), and the Southern Christian Leadership Conference (SCLC), respectively—assumed control over what was now being called the "Meredith March." In the days ahead, the march grew exponentially as it continued down Highway 51, which pierced the flat alluvial plain of the Delta.[6]

Confederate monuments had not been the object of civil rights protests in the 1960s, but as marchers entered each county seat, they often coalesced around those statues erected either on the courthouse lawn or in the center of town. There, the central symbol of racial inequality that had dominated the local landscape for generations now stood facing the movement for racial equality. African Americans, especially those black southerners most affected by the racism of local whites, were now there to reclaim the public square for themselves, asserting the rights of American citizenship. They instinctively knew and understood the history and meaning behind these statues. Granite and bronze memorials might technically be "silent," but metaphorically they spoke volumes about white supremacy in these communities. When the Meredith March entered Grenada, Mississippi, in mid-June 1966, the significance of Confederate monuments as symbols of inequality became indisputable.

The town of Grenada and the surrounding county of the same name were heavily segregated. It was a place where less than 20 percent of African Americans—who were the majority of the population—were registered to vote. They remained poor, were refused jobs in local factories, and had no access to the library or the swimming pool, and schools were not yet desegregated. Grenada was exactly the place where the Meredith March could make a difference.[7]

On June 14, over 200 marchers, black and white, spilled into the little town and made their way downtown along Main Street. They were joined by several hundred locals, and together they sang

When the Meredith March reached Grenada, Mississippi, on
June 14, 1966, hundreds of people joined the group, which coalesced
around the town's Confederate monument.
(Courtesy Bettmann/Getty Images)

freedom songs. After combining forces, the column of marchers
headed directly to the Confederate monument, which predictably
sat in the town square. Grenada's monument, erected by the UDC
in 1910, was of a lone Confederate soldier; the pedestal on which
it stood displayed a bas-relief of Jefferson Davis on one side. Since
its dedication, local whites annually observed Confederate Memorial Day at the monument, extolling the men who had fought to
keep the system of slavery intact. Yet that day in 1966 was not
about celebrating but confronting the Confederacy.

The crowd gathered around the monument and vocalized a
new vision for their community, one free from white supremacy.
A few of them even raised clenched fists in the air—the symbol of
Black Power. As horrified local whites looked on, Robert Green,

representing the SCLC, climbed onto the monument to plant an American flag above the image of Jefferson Davis and declared, "We're tired of seeing rebel flags. Give me the flag of the United States, the flag of freedom." George Raymond, a CORE field secretary, climbed onto the monument next and, pointing to the likeness of Jefferson Davis, referred to him as "the joker up there."[8] The crowd responded with cheers.

Later that evening, Martin Luther King Jr. joined the marchers, and he also took to the steps of the Confederate monument. King was there to negotiate concessions from local government, which included the hiring of five black registrars to register new voters and desegregating the library and public schools. King's spirits were lifted by what he saw in Grenada, which was one of the earliest recorded examples of a racial justice protest converging around a Confederate monument and a harbinger of those seen decades later. And over the next few days the town saw a dramatic increase in voter registration. As the march continued deeper into the Delta, white residents in Greenwood, Mississippi, however, prepared not only for the onslaught of protesters but to protect the town's Confederate monument from the kind of "desecration" they believed occurred in Grenada.

The march entered LeFlore County on June 17, led by King, Carmichael, and Hosea Williams. But as they walked onto the courthouse grounds, they were stopped by policemen and told to keep off the grass. Behind the uniformed men stood the Confederate monument, dedicated by the UDC in 1918. Local officials had taken the additional step of protecting the monument by forcing eight black prisoners from Parchman, the state penitentiary, to surround the statue, a tactic that was also used in Belzoni, Mississippi.[9] Posting black prisoners to protect a monument to the Lost Cause was an insult not only to the marchers but also to the local black community. Hosea Williams, an aide to King, shouted to white officers, "The only reason I'm not going onto that statue today is because you will beat these poor boys when they are back in jail." He knew that while these men were being used as pawns to defend the monument, the state penitentiary was notorious for its mistreatment of prisoners, the majority of whom were black men.[10]

Martin Luther King Jr. and Andrew Young took to the steps of the Confederate monument in Grenada, Mississippi, on the evening of June 14, 1966, in support of the Meredith March and to encourage voter registration. (Courtesy National Portrait Gallery, Smithsonian Institution; © Family of Charmian Reading)

After what many Mississippi whites believed was a "desecration" of the
Confederate monument in Grenada, Mississippi, officials in LeFlore
County brought in black prisoners from Parchman, the state's penitentiary,
to guard the Confederate monument in Greenwood in June 1966.
(Courtesy of Alabama Department of Archives and History)

Later in June 1966, after the Meredith March left Greenwood,
the same Parchman prisoners were sent to protect the Confederate
monument in Belzoni, Mississippi. (Courtesy Jo Freeman)

The "freedom march," as King described it, eventually made its way to Mississippi's state capital. Along the way the number of marchers ebbed and flowed from as few as 30 to over 1,000, but when the march finally arrived in Jackson on June 26, a crowd of 12,000 gathered. James Meredith had rejoined the march earlier, but by now it had grown into something larger than even he had envisioned.[11] While King had asked marchers to resist using Stokely Carmichael's slogan, "Black Power," because he believed it ran counter to the cause of integration, the chant of "Black Power! Black Power!" rang through the air as the crowd grew in size. As participants sang and shouted, the *New York Times* reported that some of them "tore occasional Confederate flags from the hands of white bystanders and ripped the pennants to shreds."[12]

The marchers had walked through downpours and blazing heat to get there. They had endured harassment and violence from white Mississippians throughout their pilgrimage as local and state law enforcement looked on. One resident in Greenwood had gone so far as to place a poisonous water moccasin in a box near where marchers set up tents for the night. But protesters were undaunted, standing tall against Confederate monuments in one town after another, rejecting the Lost Cause narrative that they represented, and reclaiming the spaces where they stood in the name of racial equality. This was *their* time.[13]

■ ■ ■

Although the Meredith March was largely focused on the vote, participants understood that combating white supremacy was linked to Confederate symbols, including monuments. The same year as the march in Mississippi, another direct challenge to Confederate monuments occurred in Alabama when students from Tuskegee Institute marched from campus into town to protest the acquittal of the white man who had murdered their classmate and friend, twenty-one-year-old Sammy Younge Jr.

Younge had grown up in Tuskegee's black middle class. Both parents were professionals: his father an occupational therapist, his mother a schoolteacher. Like many middle-class African Americans from the town, Sammy received a strong secondary education and was expected to pursue a college degree. First he joined the U.S. Navy, but health complications cut his service short after less than three years, so he enrolled at Tuskegee Institute after his return home. Ever restless, he rarely came to class but was drawn to the work of SNCC. Though he had passed as white most of his life, he embraced his race through SNCC, registered voters in nearby Brownsville, and even traveled to Ruleville, Mississippi, where he met activist Fannie Lou Hamer and briefly worked to register voters for the Mississippi Freedom Democratic Party. Still, according to friends and family, his enthusiasm for SNCC sometimes waned, perhaps because the frustrations of working for the movement exhausted him or he simply had a wanderlust for something even more meaningful. Regardless, the militancy of SNCC's approach to civil rights kept his attention and clearly influenced how he confronted racism in day-to-day life.[14]

On the night of Monday, January 3, 1966, Younge stopped by a gas station to use the restroom. He was met by the white station attendant, sixty-eight-year-old Marvin Segrest, who pointed him to the back to use the "Negro" bathroom. According to affidavits, Younge had a verbal confrontation with Segrest and asked him if he had ever heard of the Civil Rights Act. The exchange became heated and eventually Segrest pulled a gun and shot Younge in the back of the head, killing him. There he lay, in the alleyway between the gas station and the bus station, until friends found him in a pool of his own blood. Segrest, who never denied shooting Younge, was arrested and charged with second-degree murder.[15]

The news of Younge's death was devastating, and at eight o'clock on Tuesday morning students at Tuskegee, organized by student government president Gwen Patton, met in Logan Hall, the school's gym, and decided to march on the town. According to Patton, "About three thousand people turned out," and it included everyone from students and faculty to people from the community. They marched into the town of Tuskegee, where Patton read a statement to the mayor and the city council at city hall that called on the mayor to do something to desegregate schools and stores and to do more than "deplore the incident." Still others, according to the *Chicago Defender*, "stood crying in a downpour outside city hall" and "demanded the President and Federal Marshals . . . insure that justice is done."[16] They continued to march and picket city hall and the county courthouse in the days ahead

Following the murder of Tuskegee University student Sammy Younge Jr.
on January 3, 1966, Frank Toland, a professor in the Department of History,
addressed students who had gathered on the grounds surrounding the
town's Confederate monument.
(Courtesy of Alabama Department of Archives and History)

and rallied on the town square around the Confederate monument, claiming the space as their own, as marchers had done during the Meredith March in Mississippi.[17]

The second Saturday following Younge's murder, students
staged a sit-in to shut down the businesses around the square.
Because of the continued marches, the town's white leaders were
losing patience and placed more police on patrol. Laura Payton, a
Tuskegee student, recalled that Sammy's childhood friends Wen-
dell "Wendy" Paris and Eldridge Burns and others "were up on
the statue out there, in the square, trying to decide if we should
get a rope and pull it down." The boycott of stores, the frenzied

activity of marchers, and the police presence led the group to hold off on ripping down the Confederate monument. Later that year, though, they would be back.[18]

According to James Forman, who served as a field director for SNCC in Alabama, "the murder of Sammy Younge marked the end of tactical nonviolence."[19] In the days and months ahead, Tuskegee students and friends of Sammy's took to the street to express their fury over what had happened to someone so young. Eventually, they would take their frustrations out on the town's Confederate monument, which Forman called a statue "erected in memory of those who fought hard to preserve slavery," echoing the letters to the *Defender* generations earlier.[20]

In November, Marvin Segrest was finally indicted for the second-degree murder of Sammy Younge Jr., though a change of venue to Lee County was approved because Segrest's attorneys didn't believe he could get a fair trial in Macon County. The real reason was that juror rolls in Macon County were majority black, and in Lee County, Segrest got an all-white jury. The trial began in Opelika, Alabama, on December 7, 1966, and within two days, Segrest was acquitted of the charges. Tuskegee students who attended the trial were devastated, even though they had anticipated the outcome. Gwen Patton screamed, "God damn!" after the verdict was read and swiftly returned with her fellow students to Tuskegee to determine their next steps. Near 10:30 P.M. around 300 students gathered once again in the school's gymnasium. They were angry and frustrated. "There was this whole fever of blackness," Patton recalled, adding, "Negritude was coming across on students." These feelings were so strong at Tuskegee that the original group of 300 grew exponentially such that, by midnight, a crowd of 2,000 had gathered.[21]

Scott B. Smith, a student leader of SNCC at Tuskegee and previously active with CORE in Chicago, spoke up: "You're not going to lynch [Marvin] Segrest. You're not going to burn his house down. So, you got to do something." According to Gwen Patton, "Scott B. said he was going to sleep downtown in front of the Confederate statue." Then a second student said he would do the same. One after another agreed with the idea until they all decided to go. On their way to the town square, Patton recalled,

When Marvin Segrest was acquitted for the murder of Sammy
Younge Jr. on December 9, 1966, Tuskegee students returned that
evening to the Confederate monument in town to register their grief and
frustration. In addition to defacing the statue with black paint, students
painted Younge's name on the side, along with the slogan "Black Power."
(Courtesy Alabama Department of Archives and History)

the march had no form or pattern, "which was beautiful." And
they did not sing freedom songs. They were angry. Instead, they
chanted, "Black Power! Black Power!"[22]

As they gathered around the Confederate monument, Scott
Smith saw that people were not of a mind to hold a vigil. They
"wanted to do something about the problem . . . so the statue was
it." Smith and Wendy Paris called on someone in the community
get them black paint, and soon a local man arrived with two cans.
They splashed the paint on the statue and smeared a yellow stripe
down the back of the soldier atop the pedestal. They also, more
pointedly, brushed "Black Power" and "Sam Younge" along the
base. According to Smith, "When the paint hit, a roar came up
from those students. Every time the brush hit, *wham*, they'd roar
again." The attack on the statue, that symbol of white supremacy

in the middle of town, did not end there. They gathered dead leaves and created brush fires around it. One young woman's pain spilled out and she shouted, "Let's get *all* the statues—not just one. Let's go all over the state and get all the statues."[23]

The cry to "get *all* the statues" was a powerful statement. The young woman, whose name we do not know, spoke volumes. While it was too dangerous for the students to take out their frustrations on local white folks, attacking the monument served as a symbolic attack on white supremacy, as well as on the man who had killed their friend. Her plea revealed her knowledge that statues existed in nearly every town in Alabama, constant reminders of racial injustice, which she linked to Younge's death. It was not something she had learned from a course in black history, although Tuskegee would soon add such courses to its curriculum following the protests. It was not something she had necessarily heard from SNCC. Like all black southerners, her education about the meaning of Confederate monuments came from the lived experience of segregation and racial violence—as attested to by Sammy Younge Jr.'s murder.[24]

■ ■ ■

Even though the pivot toward Black Power and militancy that Stokely Carmichael and SNCC represented captured hearts and minds in Mississippi and Alabama in 1966, the fact was that white southerners, especially those in Deep South states, fiercely resisted change to the status quo. And while African American students from historically black colleges and universities risked their lives registering voters, white students demonstrated their continued dedication to the Lost Cause. The Kappa Alpha Order, the fraternity that counted Confederate general Robert E. Lee as its "spiritual founder," thrived on southern university campuses. Across the region, they held annual "Old South Balls," where men dressed in Confederate uniforms and women in hoop skirts. As part of the festivities, the fraternity leaders would send letters to politicians announcing their "secession" from the United States for a twenty-four-hour period. The first annual Old South Ball in North Carolina, for example, was held in Raleigh in 1949, where members of Kappa Alpha chapters from the University of North Carolina (UNC), Duke, Wake Forest, and North Carolina State staged a parade down Fayetteville Street before attending the ball in Memorial Auditorium, which was bedecked with Confederate flags. In advance, they sent letters to Governor Kerr Scott about their intention to "secede." A similar scene played out in Charlotte in 1958, where the chapters marched through the main streets of the city before holding a "secession ceremony" in front of the Mecklenburg County Courthouse. And for an hour, Trade Street became "Confederate Boulevard." These sorts of rituals not only maintained the Lost Cause but perpetuated racial hierarchies at southern universities.

The impulse to memorialize the Old South remained strong on southern campuses throughout the 1960s, even as the student sit-in movement drew attention to humiliating racial inequalities. In 1969 in Chapel Hill, North Carolina, where the memory of sit-ins and white supremacist violence was still fresh, UNC's Kappa Alpha members held ceremonies for "Old South Weekend" with a march across campus, some on foot and others on horseback, headed directly toward the Confederate monument known as "Silent Sam."[25] The *Daily Tar Heel* reported that "some fifty Southern Gentlemen and their belles" began their ceremonies at the base of Silent Sam. Henry Wells, the Kappa Alpha president, climbed onto the steps of the monument, where he spoke to the crowd. "We are here to celebrate the grace and charm of the Old South" and "take time to relive the spirit of our great heritage," he began. Sandy McClamroch, Chapel Hill's mayor, greeted the men and presented them with a key to the city "in keeping with the day of Old South Weekend." In return, Wells gave the mayor a bottle of "Rebel Yell" bourbon. After the exchange of Lost Cause sentiments next to Silent Sam and "in celebration of the secession," the student paper reported, everyone "retired to the mayor's plantation for beer . . . and the campus of UNC was once again reassured that the protectors of the southern tradition are still kicking."[26]

The performance of neo-Confederate traditions alongside the monument erected to honor student-soldiers who fought in a war to defend and perpetuate the institution of slavery spoke volumes about the university, its administration, and the town of Chapel Hill. All three institutions were complicit, and continued to be for years to come, in the perpetuation of a mythology with real implications for African American students on campus. The reanimation of Silent Sam, a bronze statue that regularly "spoke" to some students such that it had been made a central part of Confederate ceremonies on campus for decades, demonstrated a willingness to defend a distorted version of history. It also represented a willful disregard for racial sensitivity on campus, and racial progress more broadly, along with a determination to adhere to rituals steeped in white supremacy. At the time of the ceremony at UNC in 1969, only 1.4% of the student body was African American, but as that percentage increased, so too did challenges to the Confederate tradition, paralleling a similar pattern that emerged in local politics as cities and towns across the South elected their first black officials since the nineteenth century.[27]

■ ■ ■

In the late 1960s, there were also indicators that Americans more broadly had no appetite for racial equality. The assassination of Dr. Martin Luther King Jr. on April 4, 1968, was a blow to the movement, and it was followed seven months later by the election of Richard M. Nixon, whose "southern strategy" to win over white southern voters proved successful enough to place him in the White House. Alabama's former governor George Wallace, the segregationist who famously stood in the schoolhouse doors to prevent integration at the University of Alabama in 1963, also made a bid for president as the candidate for the American Independent Party. While he surely appealed to rural whites across the South, his candidacy also appealed to blue-collar workers in the North. Although Wallace only won 46 electoral college votes, all from states in the former Confederacy, he was on the ballot in every state and garnered nearly 10 million votes. Despite the loss, he considered his candidacy a success. The Associated Press reported that when Wallace was asked what he planned to do next, he replied, "I'm going to sit around the courthouse and the Confederate monument in Clayton," his hometown. It was a telling statement.[28]

As the 1970s began, the Lost Cause held firm, and there was no greater demonstration of that fact than what occurred on May 9, 1970, when the largest Confederate memorial ever created was dedicated in Stone Mountain, Georgia, just outside of Atlanta. The granite carving of Robert E. Lee, Stonewall Jackson, and Jefferson Davis—a project first initiated in 1916 by the Georgia United Daughters of the Confederacy—was welcomed by national and state politicians and neo-Confederate stalwarts alike. Organizers invited President Richard Nixon to give the dedication speech, but he sent Vice President Spiro Agnew in his place. With the dramatic backdrop of Lee, Jackson, and Davis on horseback behind him, the vice president addressed the crowd of 10,000 with a speech focused on what a "new South" should try to be. "This new South rejects old grievances and the old political appeals to the worst in all. This new South embraces the future and presses forward with a robust economy fueled by industrial development," he began. He spoke about setting aside the "evils of sectionalism," adding, "Just as the South cannot afford to discriminate against any of its own people, the rest of the nation cannot afford to discriminate against the South."[29] Such remarks stood in stark contrast to his own presence at the dedication, which served as an official endorsement of a memorial that had long been a site of Ku Klux Klan activity.

The State of Georgia purchased the Stone Mountain memorial from the Venable family in 1958 for approximately $2 million in order to develop a state park around it.[30] But James Venable, a sixty-five-year-old attorney and the Imperial Wizard of the Ku Klux Klan, boycotted the dedication when he learned that an African American minister was on the program, calling it "an offense" to the memory of Lee, Jackson, and Davis "to have a Negro at the event." Venable was also quoted as saying, "The war was fought over the question of slavery and it is improper for a member of [the minister's] race to take part in the program." While his racism was palpable, the statement that "the war was fought over the question of slavery" ran counter to Lost Cause rhetoric that it had been about states' rights. Nonetheless, Venable appeared pleased to have Agnew deliver the speech, rather than Nixon, because, he said, "I share his views on college students and professors running amok and all that communistic, socialistic stuff."[31]

Even though the pace of monument building slowed in the 1970s, monuments continued to make the news over the next decade, often as part of Confederate Memorial Day ceremonies or when local newspapers waxed nostalgic about the history of their town's monument. The UDC still garnered publicity, but more frequently coverage of its activities took up space on the women's social pages. More importantly, however, political representation was undergoing significant change across the region. The increased voter registration that had taken place since 1965, in fact, bore significant results as African Americans, many of whom had developed leadership experience in the civil rights movement, were elected to office. These new representatives asserted their status as public officials to confront Confederate symbols on government property for being an insult to black citizens. As they did, they demonstrated that they were conversant with the role Confederate symbols had long played in the history of the South.

■ ■ ■

On Memorial Day in 1974, Marian Rawls, a seventy-six-year-old voice teacher and officer in her local chapter of the UDC in Portsmouth, Virginia, helped decorate the Confederate monument in her town with Confederate flags, primarily battle flags. It was an annual ritual the UDC had performed ever since the monument, which sat at the intersection of Court and High Streets, was dedicated in 1893. Such rituals were treated as completely inoffensive and even patriotic for years, but this time was different. The first African American elected to the city council, James Holley, spoke up at the city council meeting immediately following Rawls's decoration of the statue to call for the flags to be taken down and replaced with American flags. The disagreement was one of the first in a series of battles taking place throughout the South over the meaning of Confederate symbols—both monuments and flags—located on city-owned property.

The forty-eight-year-old Holley was a World War II veteran, a highly educated dentist, and an active participant in the civil rights movement in Portsmouth. Before winning election to the council in 1968, he had played an important role in desegregating the city's schools, libraries, and other publicly funded facilities. Like other black veterans, he believed in the symbolism of the U.S. flag, not that of the Confederacy. Yet, in newspaper accounts of events that year, Marian Rawls was held up as a heroine for her Lost Cause stance. The *Fort Lauderdale News* published the

Monuments and the Battle for First-Class Citizenship

UPI's coverage of the battle under the title "Brave Woman Fights City Fathers to Decorate Monument," while the *Kingsport Times* in Tennessee referred to it as the "Confederate Battle of Marian Rawls." As Rawls explained, the Daughters had voted, as they had done in previous years, to place flags around the monument. When the city council decided to have them removed, Rawls told the city manager, "Those flags better not be touched," and vowed to members of the city council, "If you take them down six times, I'll put them back seven times." The *Fort Lauderdale News* version of the article described Councilman Holley as "a black" and also reported that the UDC had posted guards around the statue to prevent the removal of Confederate flags, noting that the city council had no say in the matter since it had "ceded the land" to the women.[32]

The Portsmouth city council, which now included black representation, won the "skirmish" with Marian Rawls. She eventually gave up her fight to place flags on the monument. Holley's protest, moreover, was not an outlier in a region that increasingly was electing black officials to public office. Just a few years after the dustup in Portsmouth, another black city councilman confronted the dedication of a new Confederate monument on the grounds of city hall in Charlotte, North Carolina. His name: Harvey Gantt.

Born in 1943 in Charleston, South Carolina, Gantt became the first black student to attend Clemson University, where he graduated with honors in 1965 with a degree in architecture. A few years later, he earned a master's degree in city planning from MIT and in 1971 moved to Charlotte, North Carolina, where he formed an architectural firm with Jeffrey Huberman. In 1974, the thirty-one-year-old Gantt filled an open seat on the city council vacated by the first black member to serve in that capacity and won an at-large seat for a two-year term that began in 1977.[33] In May of that year, a new Confederate monument was placed on the grounds of city hall. Clearly, the civil rights movement hadn't stopped such monuments from being raised, but the Voting Rights Act now meant that African Americans' views about Confederate symbols in their community could finally find representation in government—and Gantt's exchanges with fellow council members, as well as with white citizens, took direct aim at the meaning of Confederate monuments. Erecting new Confederate memorials and markers had gone unchallenged for decades, such that the process for adding new ones seemed almost assured, but Gantt's presence on the city council changed that dynamic.

In the fall of 1976, Larry Walker, a thirty-year-old Vietnam veteran who claimed Confederate ancestry, decided that Charlotte needed a more prominent monument to honor soldiers from Mecklenburg County who had fought for the Confederacy. Two memorials already existed—an obelisk erected in Elmwood Cemetery in 1887 and a granite marker placed adjacent to American Legion Memorial Stadium in 1929 following a reunion of Confederate veterans. The latter paid homage to Confederate soldiers while also honoring them for having "preserved the Anglo-Saxon civilization of the South." Walker was unsatisfied. "They're in obscure places," he said, whereas "practically every Southern town, regardless of its size, has such a monument prominently placed." He wanted the same for the monument he had in mind and approached city officials.[34]

Mayor John Belk forwarded the issue to the city manager, Paul Bobo, who, according to Walker, gave him permission to erect a monument in front of city hall in an area where other historical monuments existed, including one honoring the doughboys of World War I. Walker, who represented what he called the "Confederate Memorial Society," began fundraising for the monument and received donations from the UDC, the Daughters of the American Revolution, and the Metrolina Retired Officers Association, among others. During the process, one of the groups suggested that he reach out to members of the city council, because he would need the council's permission. Among those Walker contacted included Councilwomen Pat Locke and Betty Chafin, as well as Councilman James Whittington. All three, he asserted, "gave their wholehearted approval of this project."[35]

But just one week before the monument was to be dedicated, some council members were only just learning about it, including Harvey Gantt. At the May 16, 1977, meeting, he called for the council to take up the motion to discuss, for the very first time, the request to place the memorial in front of city hall. Larry Walker stood up and laid out the timeline of events, which included taking proper steps to contact city officials and getting permission from Paul Bobo. He also explained that council members Locke, Chafin, and Whittington had all endorsed the project. Then he addressed Gantt directly, telling him that there was no intention on his part or that of the other organizations "of any sort of racial slur" or that "we feel to be of a superior race, or anything of that nature," then added, "We feel that our culture of the South should not be suppressed." His use of "our culture" clearly did not include Gantt, despite the fact that both men, who were approximately the same age, had grown up in the same region.[36]

As it turned out, the city council had already approved a proposal to erect a monument to Dr. Martin Luther King Jr. in the city's Marshall Park. Walker used that fact to then try to equate the two, saying that because those individuals affiliated with the Confederate Memorial Society had not opposed the monument to King, there should be "reciprocal treatment." This would become a common refrain among southern whites who regarded any commemoration of Martin Luther King Jr. as sufficient in representing the black citizens in their communities and thus a justification for protecting Confederate monuments.

Councilman Gantt began by pointing out how he, the sole black representative on the city council, had been cut out of the process. "Apparently some members of the Council have been kept in the dark with regard to Mr. Walker's efforts to establish this memorial," he said, expressing that he was "somewhat appalled that at least three or four members of the Council have given . . . [their] tacit approval." As for the effort to honor Dr. King, Gantt told Walker, "either you have been misled or do not understand the City's policy," since that action had been approved by the city council while the Confederate monument had not.[37]

He then spoke to what he regarded as the legacy of such memorials and their meaning for the black community. "It seems to me that in a city that has 90,000 black citizens, one has to question whether a monument, placed to honor the Confederate dead, is part of a history that I and [other black citizens] want to account for to our children," Gantt said. "I do not think a monument placed in a prominent place in this city, with the diverse population that it has, that is erected to glorify soldiers who fought in defense of slavery . . . is right," he proclaimed, "and I will say this as loud and clear as I possibly can."[38]

Gantt was sympathetic to the fact that Walker had been misled by some of the council members, who also had kept the information about the monument from him. It was already in place in anticipation of a dedication later that week, and, Gantt rightly noted, permission was now being sought "after the fact." Still, the councilman asked for clarification of the policy, very likely to demonstrate to everyone that a backroom deal had been struck with Walker that ignored city policy. Another councilman moved to place this item on the agenda for the following week's meeting, which carried.[39]

Walker asked if he should call off the dedication. Mayor Belk replied that the council had not approved the monument and would have to do so before a dedication could take place. But the monument was already on the grounds of city hall, and even the mayor had an invitation to attend. Council members were now caught in a web of their own creation and one by one began backtracking. James Whittington "did not remember Mr. Walker calling him" and then threw the city manager under the bus, stating that if "Mr. Bobo gave him permission to erect the monument here, he gave it without the knowledge of the Council." The mayor denied receiving a letter from Walker, too, and also pointed the finger at Paul Bobo. Councilwoman Locke chimed in that she "did not remember talking to Mr. Walker" about the statue either.[40]

Larry Walker was stunned—so much so that his wife got up to address the council. Her husband, she insisted, "has been working on this project for months." He had taken the appropriate steps "to preserve a little history" and couldn't believe how members of the Charlotte City Council "can sit there and try to get out of what they told him . . . because of one comment negating this," clearly referencing Gantt's disapproval. When her husband regained his composure, he asked, "What am I supposed to do with a 2,000-pound monument if I don't get Council's approval?" Then Mrs. Walker spoke again to say that it was likely that some of the council members had ancestors who fought for the Confederacy and hoped that they would "have a little more pride . . . than that." Walker later told a reporter for the *Charlotte Observer*, "I wouldn't have done it if I thought Mr. Gantt would object." Then, he fumed, "But after all, he has his Martin Luther King monument to his cultural heritage," adding, "I ought to be able to have a monument to my heritage which is, after all, the cultural heritage of the majority, which is white Americans."[41]

On Saturday, May 21, a crowd of 100 attended the dedication of the Confederate monument in front of city hall, which went ahead as planned. Despite being invited, Mayor Belk was a no-show after explaining in the previous council meeting he would attend "if he was going to be in town." In the wake of the controversy the monument had caused, he was conveniently unavailable. Still, the issue did not go away. On Monday, May 23, the city council returned to the discussion of the memorial placed by Walker's group.

Councilman Joe Withrow began the meeting with a motion to approve the monument's placement in front of city hall, which was seconded by James Whittington, the member who had already given tacit approval the year before. Larry Walker then addressed the council. He reiterated the details of the previous week, offering letters proving that the city manager had given him permission. Walker also defended the meaning of the memorial as "nothing more or less than freedom of speech and recognition of historical fact and cultural heritage," which, he claimed, was "the same right" given to supporters of the Martin Luther King monument. He additionally offered a letter signed by junior high school students that supported his cause and took pleasure in noting that "fifty percent of the students . . . are black," suggesting that these students understood the issue.[42]

Mike Ridge, a monument supporter, spoke next. He pointed to the recent celebration of the nation's bicentennial and suggested that there was no difference between Revolutionary ancestors and Confederate ancestors in that both fights included a preservation of the institution of slavery. If one could be commemorated, he reasoned, then why not the other? Another monument supporter, Jim Richardson, reiterated a statement made by Walker the previous week, claiming "no racial slur was intended in any way." Spero Calos, representing the local Metrolina Retired Officers Association, a group of former military officers who supported the monument, touted how his association, which annually gave a medal to the outstanding ROTC student, gave that honor to a black student at Independence High School. Clearly, both Richardson and Calos wanted to dismiss any notion that they were racists.[43]

Harry Simmons, another citizen, told council members that he was there after seeing the televised meeting from the previous week. He was angry about how much attention the media had given the issue. "It is really amazing when we can turn out the news media for something as insignificant as the discussion of a monument when we have more important things in our community," he fumed. Simmons also wanted to prove he wasn't being racist by adding that he had given money to the King memorial and "participated in a protest against segregation in the 1960s." Still, he complained, "I am tired of hearing about slavery in the South," then pivoted to an explanation of his Confederate ancestry. He ended his rant by arguing, "To say that the Confederacy represents slavery is to accept the same type of bias that branded 'the only good Indian is a dead Indian.'"[44]

Shirley Simms, a UDC leader, also spoke. She was dumbfounded by the controversy, calling it "the height of silliness." The fact of what she called the "Confederate war" could not be changed; "our people have fought in it." Simms regarded the placement of the Confederate memorial in front of city hall as a benign act. "They wanted a monument where people could see it," she said. "Now they have had all this faction and trouble over a 'tempest in a teapot.'" Simms then repeated the Lost Cause line that had circulated among white southerners since 1865. "The war was not fought for slavery, the war was fought for states' rights," she said, adding, "which many of us still believe in."[45]

After listening to several speakers trotting out the Lost Cause and attempting to deflect charges of racism, Councilman Harvey Gantt addressed the room. "I would really like to acknowledge all of the phone calls and letters I received regarding this monument," he began; "I've been quite enlightened by both sides of this question." As for the letter signed by the eighth-grade class that Walker referenced, Gantt noted that "apparently the class has a view of history that I did not get while I was growing up, and I'm enlightened by that." He had received several calls and letters telling him he was "denying history," to which he responded, "I'm enlightened by that, also." And, "The charges of racism and bias on my part [are] indeed enlightening to me."[46]

But Gantt disagreed with Walker about the history behind the monument, and he made that disagreement plain. "I feel the war . . . had everything to do with a way of life that [would have] subjugated me and subjugated [other] Americans," he said. In reference to the idea of brave southern soldiers, mentioned often in the meeting, Gantt replied, "I shudder to think . . . what this country would be like had they won." He then drew attention to the moment in which they were all living, when only a few years earlier, black Americans were still fighting for the right to vote. "I find it remarkable that people expect that I would want to, in fact, glorify that war," he exclaimed, telling Walker, "There is no way that I can forget that history."[47]

Gantt also made it clear that, even if other speakers were deluded by the mythology of the Lost Cause, he certainly knew the history of how slavery shaped the South and the nation. He pointed out how "a tremendous amount of energy and resources" had been spent over the previous decade to try and rectify "some of the injustices perpetuated in the founding of this entire country going back two hundred years." He also addressed the charges of partiality, telling Walker's group, "I am sorry that we have citizens that think my opinion is biased against their grandfathers, great grandfathers, and others, but I also feel that we have, in history, paid great attention to the Confederate war dead," a clear reference to the hundreds of monuments and markers scattered throughout the South, including in Charlotte.[48]

As the only black council member, Gantt took pains to explain to his white colleagues and citizens what the history espoused by Walker's group meant to black southerners, referencing his own lived experience. "I grew up in Charleston and all of my life I viewed Confederate monuments and other symbols of the South," he began, "and that does not change my impression of what the war was essentially fought for." On the question of states' rights, he continued, "That question was central only because [the Confederacy] sought to perpetuate a way of life that had as its central focus an economic system dependent on the work of slaves." In essence, Gantt rejected the Lost Cause narrative about the meaning of Confederate monuments claimed by Walker and others.[49]

One of the concerns being expressed by several white citizens, including members of Walker's group, was that somehow the significance of placing a Confederate monument in front of city hall was a matter of equity and diversity given that the city council had approved placing the King monument on city-owned property. Gantt pushed back. The monument to King and the Confederate monument were "not analogous," he argued, because what "Dr. King fought for cannot be defined along the lines of race—he sought to fulfill the Constitution that has never been fulfilled in over two hundred years." When the city council approved the King monument, it was intended to be "representative of a kind of New South," Gantt explained, "a kind of new healing mechanism" in hopes that such healing would "spread throughout Charlotte."[50]

Gantt concluded by referencing the UDC leader's assertion that the question of the monument on the grounds of city hall was unimportant. "You may say [it] is a 'silly' thing, as the lady said earlier, but it is symbolic," he explained, adding, "It is symbolic in the sense that we need to do things that will heal the community."[51]

In his most pointed and poignant argument about the monument, Gantt drew from the history of racial inequality in the South: "In 1923, it might have been just a matter of course to put a monument out on the lawn of City Hall, but you did not have black citizens in this community voting, they were not participants as first class citizens, and I don't think anyone would deny that." He closed by returning to the present scars left by this history: "In 1977, we need to say to the world that all of our citizens are first class and the symbolic effect of a Council that glorifies a war fought 100 years ago to defend a system that would deny first class citizenship to a substantial portion of its citizenry is very important—it cuts deeply."[52]

Harvey Gantt had spoken with passion and eloquence, marshalling such a mastery of history and the importance of symbolism in a modern context that some of the other council members were clearly shamefaced. Yet Councilman Louis Davis told Gantt that he approved of the monument and, unironically, borrowed words from Abraham Lincoln, proclaiming, "My vote is cast with malice toward none and charity for all." Councilman Neil Williams was moved by Gantt's comments about healing the community and suggested adding "USA" to the monument. Although he had not seen it, as a Republican he felt that a quote from Lincoln might have been appropriate to add to the memorial, including the one shared by Davis, and made a motion to that effect. Gantt seconded it, but both were outvoted. Then, council members voted on the original motion, which was to allow the Confederate monument to be placed in front of the city hall—a full two weeks after it was dedicated. The motion carried; Gantt cast the only "nay" vote.[53]

Charlotteans continued their discussion of the monument in the days ahead. In a piece titled "We're Not Big on Statues: And It's a Little Late for This One," *Charlotte Observer* columnist Harriet Doar mocked locals for their sudden concern over Confederate memorials. She wondered "why Charlotte did not see fit to put up a first-class Confederate monument in the center of town by the turn of the century, like other towns." She noted that the city had taken no notice of Zebulon Vance, North Carolina's Civil War governor who had lived in Charlotte for twenty-eight years (although in 1997 a high school would be named in his honor). "The house where the last full Confederate Cabinet meeting was held fell to Sears, Roebuck, and Jefferson Davis's headquarters only recently crumbled into a parking lot," Doar wrote. She suggested, sympathetically, "If I were Harvey Gantt, elected by a large cross-section of voters, I think I'd have trouble keeping a straight face at this belated Confederate recognition."[54]

Several readers railed against Gantt for questioning Confederate tradition while exposing their own racial attitudes. In the "Observer Forum," letters about the monument debate appeared under the heading "South Fought for Its Way of Life." Beverly Bertram began her letter defending the Confederate states, which she believed "fought not to protect slavery but their way of life." Bill Holder wrote, "It seems that Harvey Gantt and his people will be morally offended by this reminder of a fight to defend slavery," and felt Gantt's sole purpose was to "blot out a segment of our history that is distasteful to him." Holder opined, "Surely Charlotte has not come to the point where ethnic opinion dictates the policy of the community." He mistakenly employed the term "ethnic" rather than "racial" and lectured that "Mr. Gantt should realize that there are many of us who feel strongly about our Southern heritage," as though Gantt was not also a southerner. Then, referencing the King memorial, Holder added, "I feel that a Civil War monument is much more indicative of this community's heritage than the statue of a minority agitator that is to adorn a central city park." Marie English offered a unique solution to the problem, writing that "if there is to be such a marker, perhaps it would be appropriate to incorporate a black band on it to signify the grief that so many people of both races sacrificed to an institution, slavery, which made money for only a few." "Monuments," she believed, served as "reminders of the horror."[55]

One reader wrote to the *Charlotte Observer* about Gantt himself. In a letter titled "Gantt Deserves Commendation," Jo Brown began, "I would like to commend Councilman Harvey Gantt on his immense dignity, strength and character regarding the controversy over the monument to the Confederate war dead." Brown, who attended the city council meetings during which the monument was discussed, expressed agreement with Gantt's central premise that "the symbolic effect of this cement slab defends second-class citizenship of blacks during the Civil War period," and, echoing the councilman, wrote, "This cuts deeply." She noted that after Gantt spoke in opposition to the monument, "he was applauded." Brown was among them. "To my surprise an elderly man sitting beside me yelped, 'What the hell are you applauding for, you moron?,'" leading her to ask, "how deep and true are the real reasons for mounting this cement slab?"[56]

While Larry Walker had his way, he never forgot the controversy that erupted. He remained bitter two years later when Harvey Gantt first became a candidate for mayor. In a letter to the *Charlotte Observer* written in September 1979, Walker challenged the notion that Gantt could be "fair to all residents." His letter returned to events of 1977 when, he claimed, "Gantt expressed violent opposition" to the Confederate monument. This bent the truth of what happened, as Gantt was very measured and civil throughout the proceedings. But the use of "violent opposition" was purposefully inflammatory, and he closed by saying, "I hope

After serving several years on the city council of Charlotte,
North Carolina, during which time he spoke out against the dedication
of a Confederate monument on the grounds of City Hall in 1977,
Harvey Gantt (*left*), seen here during his inauguration in 1983,
became the city's first black mayor.
(Courtesy Charlotte Corporate Communications Records,
J. Murrey Atkins Library, UNC Charlotte)

the voters will remember this incident, when Harvey Gantt voted his own prejudice and against equal rights for all." The tactic of employing the language associated with civil rights was rich, indeed, and an omen of the future.[57]

CODA

Six years after the battle over the Confederate monument played out, in 1983, Harvey Gantt became Charlotte's first black mayor. James Holley became the first black mayor of Portsmouth, Virginia, in 1984. And because of the Voting Rights Act of 1965, more and more figures like Gantt and Holley were bringing the fight to the halls of power in southern cities and states. Yet living monuments to the Lost Cause, such as elder statesmen like Jesse Helms and Strom Thurmond, as well as young men like Larry Walker and Kappa Alpha fraternity members, continued to represent a point of view that encouraged a defense of Confederate symbols. Despite gains, black elected officials throughout the South were regularly confronted with the monuments and battle flags that either stood or flew in opposition to racial equality. That opposition eventually coalesced into a neo-Confederate movement, proving that the Lost Cause tradition had never died; rather, it reemerged and pulled Americans without any Confederate ancestors at all into its clutches.

5

DEBATING
REMOVAL
IN A
CHANGING
POLITICAL
LANDSCAPE

During the 1966 Meredith March, groups of marchers occasionally peeled off the main route to register voters in other towns throughout Mississippi. In late June some of them headed to Philadelphia, the place where civil rights workers Michael Schwerner, James Chaney, and Andrew Goodman had been brutally murdered two years earlier. It was a bold move and one that reflected SNCC's strategy to confront white intransigence to voter registration head on, even in Philadelphia. As often happened during civil rights marches across the South, white southerners met and taunted participants with Confederate battle flags—and not for the sake of "heritage." Gordon Grogan, the president of the Jackson chapter of Americans for the Preservation of the White Race, confirmed as much in 1966, when he urged Philadelphia's local white citizens to respond to the arrival of activists by flying Confederate flags from public buildings, from their homes, and from their car aerials—a tactic he also called for in Jackson. Grogan said out loud what had long been understood. "If there is anything that seems to bother these agitators," he said, "flying the Confederate flag is it." Such obstructive tactics would become very familiar in the decades that followed.[1]

Some two decades later, in the 1980s, the region witnessed the beginning of the NAACP's first battles to remove Confederate flags from statehouses in the South. And while the focus was on flags placed on the grounds of government, the group's efforts also drew attention to other Confederate symbols, namely monuments. Often, it was the combination of a battle flag stationed alongside a monument adjacent to a courthouse that led to the push to remove both from public grounds. Once again, local black elected officials and leaders pressed their communities on the issue of removal, which led to public debates among black and white southerners about history, heritage, and meaning.

As the twentieth century drew to a close, some of the earliest efforts to place what would later be called "counter monuments" were under way, the best known being the statue of Arthur Ashe in Richmond. Local debates continued into the new century as communities considered how to counteract the presence of Confederate monuments, which by then had occupied public spaces for over a hundred years. Very often, they evoked nostalgia among white southerners, who in several cases raised the alarm about their deterioration. This led to efforts to restore the statues, sometimes with state and even federal funds. Black southerners, on the other hand, continued to register their contempt for monuments and sought ways to diminish the power of these statues in their communities.

Between 1980 and 2015, public debates over the meaning and value of Confederate symbols waxed and waned. Southern branches of the NAACP initiated protests against the Confederate flags that flew over state capitols and were incorporated into state flags. That effort gained enough momentum to create change while also drawing attention to the existence of Confederate monuments on government property. It was during this period that discussions about removing monuments first began. Success in this area alarmed many southern whites and led to the creation of a neo-Confederate movement, which sought to protect these symbols while also fomenting a backlash against the racial progress that allowed discussions about removing monuments to even exist. Beginning in the 1990s, this backlash gathered sufficient strength to become influential on the national political stage, slowing the tide of change around Confederate symbols. By 2010, increasingly prominent politicians were employing talking points around protecting monuments for the sake of defending "heritage." Nonetheless, efforts to alter the regional landscape— through monument removal, via counter monuments, or by providing historical context—continued. Public debates around the issue once again illustrated that there was no common ground on which to compromise.

■ ■ ■

As the 1980s ushered in the Reagan Revolution and the rise of the New Right, southern communities continued to tangle with the Confederate tradition as black southerners challenged symbols they had long regarded as insulting to their race. What gave these challenges more traction, of course, was the increased representation of African Americans in local politics and on college campuses. White southerners could no longer ignore how black citizens regarded Confederate symbols, even as they persisted in defending the presence of flags and monuments as honoring southern heritage.

While monuments and flags were often debated locally, in 1987 the Southeast Regional Conference of the NAACP made the issue a region-wide battle by passing a resolution calling for the removal of Confederate flags above the statehouses in South Carolina and Alabama. The resolution also demanded that the state flags of Georgia and Mississippi, which incorporated the Confederate battle flag, be changed. This effort predated the NAACP's national resolution on Confederate flags by twelve years. As Savannah, Georgia, native Earl Shinhoster, the Southeast Regional's executive director, told the press, "We don't need . . . the Confederate flag as a reminder of days gone by or days that should have been buried." The regional resolution was even more emphatic, referring to the flags as symbols of "divisiveness, racial animosity and an insult to black people throughout the region."[2]

There had never been such a direct challenge to the Confederate battle flag, and it brought the issue of Confederate symbols into broader public discussions in the states targeted by the resolution, as well as in national newspapers. In 1987, David Treadwell of the *Los Angeles Times* examined the issue in an article titled "Symbol of Racism? Confederate Flag: Battle Still Raging." As Treadwell noted, the reaction of black southerners to this particular symbol "underscores a continuing problem for the South in the region's attempt to create a truly biracial society." The flag was not the only concern. "Symbols and memorials of the South's Confederate heritage," he continued, "abound below the Mason-Dixon line." The flag, printed on everything from hats to beach towels, was just one reminder of the South's Confederate tradition. There was also the singing of "Dixie" at college football games, as well as holidays that commemorated Confederate heroes Robert E. Lee and Jefferson Davis. Hundreds of Confederate monuments, too, added to what Treadwell accurately described as a "source of never-ending friction between whites and blacks."[3]

The *Los Angeles Times* article was reprinted widely across the South and sparked debate in the pages of state newspapers. Alabama state representative Alvin Holmes, who was quoted in the article and expressed sentiments shared by many black southerners, said that the Confederate battle flag on top of the state capitol was "the flag of a defunct and disgraced nation, one that wanted to hold my forebears in slavery." What he said next, however, alarmed white southerners not only in Alabama but across the South: "Every Confederate flag or symbol of the Confederacy should be barred from Alabama and every other part of the country." Many people took this statement to mean that Confederate monuments also had to go.[4]

In Alabama and South Carolina, letters to the editor suggested that the NAACP's resolution was going to lead to worse "disasters" than taking down the flag. In a letter to the *Alabama Journal*, Allen

Steed of Montgomery defended the flag as only partially about slavery and saw removal as a potentially devastating trend. "The logic behind the NAACP's desire to remove the flag," he wrote, "would lead to the removal of state funding to or support of any monument to the Confederacy." South Carolinian E. M. Moore made a similar argument in his letter to the *Greenville News*. "I sincerely fear that removal of the flag would open the floodgates for an onslaught against our Southern heritage," he worried, "the likes of which we have never seen before." Such slippery-slope rhetoric suggested a white heritage under siege. "After removal of the flag and the playing of 'Dixie,'" he continued, "these people will probably . . . try and have our Confederate monuments and plaques removed." Just as had happened in Charlotte, North Carolina, a decade earlier, the writer's use of the term "our Southern heritage" and "these people" implied a heritage that denied that African Americans, too, were southerners. In Georgia, state representative Denmark Groover, who in 1956 led the charge to incorporate the battle flag into the state flag, dismissed the flag resolution altogether. "We can't remove everything from public life that is perceived to be offensive to every group," he said. "If so, the first thing we should do is go around the state knocking down all the Confederate monuments."[5]

Nowhere did the association between the battle flag and Confederate monuments reach such a pitched battle than in Shreveport, Louisiana. On the courthouse grounds of Caddo Parish—a parish so notorious for its history of racial violence that it once held the nickname "Bloody Caddo"—the battle flag flew on a pole adjacent to the monument that was erected by the United Daughters of the Confederacy in 1905. The flag, however, did not join the monument until 1951, during the early years of the modern civil rights movement. For two years, 1987 to 1989, the community and the Caddo Parish Commission debated the propriety of both symbols on the grounds of local government. The editorial board of the *Shreveport Journal* would go a step further, giving Shreveport the distinction of becoming the first place in the nation where monument removal was formally put on the table.[6]

In Caddo Parish as elsewhere, the rising tide of black voting power was the backdrop for the debate over Confederate sym-

The Caddo Parish Confederate monument, dedicated in Shreveport, Louisiana, in 1905, continued to be celebrated by neo-Confederates in 2011, after years of debate over its removal that stretched back to 1987. (AP Photo/Val Horvath Davidson, The Times)

bols. On January 1, 1987, the *Shreveport Journal* blared the headline "Shreveport: Majority Black by 2000," and while the paper examined the changing demographics of the town, another story in the same edition suggested that editors were also thinking about the issue of the battle flag as a symbol of racial unrest. In an article titled "Rebel Flag Evokes Range of Emotions," black and white citizens of the city were interviewed about the flag's meaning. Some blacks were so offended by the flag and monument grouping in front of the parish courthouse that they refused to enter the building from that side. As one black Shreveport native commented, "Any black person knows what that flag means. It is the symbol of white supremacy. It is to black people what the swastika is to Jews." Members of the local Sons of Confederate Veterans obviously took a different view. Charles Moore did not understand what all the fuss was about, asking, "Is it the coloreds again? Anyone who says that flag is about racism is a hypocrite." Another SCV member suggested, "Let's forget about slavery," and then, speaking of Union troops, added, "How would you feel if someone came to burn your house, kill your family, and take your slaves?"[7]

At a meeting of the Caddo Parish Commission, members of a group called the Coalition of Concerned Citizens asked that the flag be taken down because it showed an "indifference" to race relations in Shreveport. UDC member Alma Garrett pushed back on the racism charge, telling those assembled, "The Confederate flag is our flag and it is what we say it is." Willie Cornelius, president of the coalition, countered. "We have a flag hanging over the halls of justice," and, he warned, "failure to handle this speedily will set this city ablaze." While there were black members of the commission who voted to take down the flag, like David Wyndon, there were not enough votes to remove it. Instead, the commission offered its preliminary approval of a monument to Martin Luther King Jr., which Wyndon pressed for, noting that he wanted to offer "something on the parish grounds to satisfy the black people."[8]

What came next likely shocked both black and white residents in Caddo Parish. In an editorial called "A Plan for Unity," the *Shreveport Journal* acknowledged the deep division over the issue. "On one side are blacks offended by the presence of a flag they view as a discredited symbol of racism, [while] on the other side are whites who believe it is just a symbol of regional legacy," the editors wrote. But they also asserted that the issue was too easily cast aside by the white majority on the parish commission. The editors acknowledged what many whites did not— that while the UDC provided the monument and the flag on the courthouse grounds, "the funds for ongoing attention to it come from the public weal and treasury"—and suggested that "even if someone with adequate means were to offer to provide support for the monument and flag en [sic] perpetuity, that still would not rectify the matter of its location on a significant public site."[9]

The editors then offered what they believed to be "a simple solution." As part of the paper's plea for unity, they recommended, "Move the flag and monument to a private plot. This would generate much good will and leave supporters of the monument a sense of direct action in having provided a safe haven for these symbols." They also warned, "A day of reckoning is coming for Shreveport's white community."

Responses from local white citizens played out in letters to the editor for over a year. "To take down the Confederate monument and flags would be an attempt to hide history," UDC member Rosemary Lee Chamberlain complained, suggesting that critics of the symbols "find another scapegoat for 'racial sensitivity.'" Eleanor Colquitt offered her two cents with an opinion that might have come from slavery defenders during the antebellum period. "I think black people should revere the hardships of their ancestors," she wrote, "since their descendants are much better off in the United States than their brothers and sisters are in Africa." Lawrence Rhodes, commander of the Arkansas Division of the SCV, threatened that attempts to move either the monument or the flag "constituted an overt act of historical censorship and cannot or will not be permitted."[10]

Two years after the *Shreveport Journal's* editorial, local whites were still furious. They called on black leaders to "address 'real' issues," including drug use, teenage pregnancy, high unemployment, and the lack of education and training—with no sense of irony that systemic racism was the root cause of these "real issues." Bennie McAdoo wrote to the *Shreveport Times*, "I for one am tired of being flogged for the sins of my ancestors. . . . You can dismantle every Confederate monument standing, burn every Rebel flag in the country, rewrite our history books and bar 'Dixie' from the airwaves, but these things will not solve your problems." Change, he argued, "must come from within your own culture." Once again, white southerners explained their defense of Confederate monuments as divided into categories of "our culture" and heritage and "your culture," which they clearly saw as inferior.[11]

Shreveport's public debate made it to the pages of *USA Today* in February 1989, where a photo of the Caddo monument accompanied an article about the South's Confederate symbols—a full two years after the *Shreveport Journal* offered its "simple solution." This concerned Hersey Wilson, vice president of the Caddo Parish Commission. "February has been an interesting month," he said. For one, David Duke, the former Grand Wizard of the Ku Klux Klan in Louisiana, had just been elected to the state legislature. Then there were the Confederate symbols still sitting squarely in front of the parish courthouse. "This is not a good image of us that the nation is seeing," Wilson lamented. There would be no progress on removal in Shreveport for the foreseeable future, and events there hinted that a nascent movement was under way to push back against political gains made by African Americans and to force compromises to protect Confederate monuments.[12]

■ ■ ■

The 1990s witnessed critical changes to the political landscape of the South, as more African Americans were elected to state and local offices. This rise in black voting power, however, did not go unnoticed and was met by an escalation of white resistance both politically and through grassroots white supremacist groups. In 1990, Charlotte, North Carolina's former mayor Harvey Gantt made an unsuccessful bid to unseat Jesse Helms in the U.S. Senate, but his strong showing—he earned 47 percent of the vote— unnerved the largely white members of the Republican Party in the South. Following the results of the 1990 U.S. Census, state legislatures began redrawing state districts, creating what were known as majority-minority districts. This form of gerrymandering, sometimes called affirmative gerrymandering, did not violate voting rights regulations. Rather, it consolidated the minority vote, limiting a black majority to one district. As political scientist Angie Maxwell explains, while these new lines ensured minority representation, "it bleached the other districts white, allowing the GOP to pick up seats fast in the South." It was a highly successful GOP strategy that ushered in a Republican majority in the House of Representatives in 1994, the first election cycle after districts were redrawn. This realignment of the South, which minimized African American representation, had consequences for the region and has led to the gerrymandered districts we currently see today. These conservative white political leaders who returned to power in the South in the 1990s and afterward, moreover, have regularly used a defense of Confederate symbols to rally constituents who fear their removal.[13]

A backlash to the rise of black political leadership as a threat to Confederate symbols, and to southern heritage more generally, was already emerging by the early 1990s. The decade also saw the rise of new white supremacist groups. The resentment over the social and cultural shift wrought by civil rights, the women's movement, and the push toward multiculturalism in the 1970s and 1980s boiled over in Alabama in 1992, when white separatists held a rally in Birmingham. According to thirty-four-year-old Bill Riccio, commander of the National Aryan Front, the group wanted to draw attention to the fact that Alabama had been "designated as a white homeland." Around sixty white separatist skinheads and Klansmen also participated in the march that coalesced around the Confederate monument in Linn Park, where they heard speeches. The men carried both Nazi and Confederate battle flags, shouted "Sieg heil!," and received police protection. Alan Galleon, the eighteen-year-old spokesman for the Confederate Hammer Skinheads, told a reporter, "Hopefully, it'll be violent."[14]

Although the Birmingham march did not erupt into violence — the only arrests were of three black men for harassment and disorderly conduct as part of a counterprotest — it was nonetheless an indication that a movement was afoot in the South among white men eager to reclaim their dominance. That they chose Alabama, which had a long history of violent opposition to racial equality, and rallied around the Confederate monument in Linn Park in the center of the city was intentional and in some ways foreshadowed events in Charlottesville, Virginia, twenty-five years later.

Two years after white separatists rallied at Birmingham's Confederate monument, and the same year that House Republicans were whisked into office to begin their "Contract with America," a new group emerged as protectors of Confederate heritage — the League of the South (LOS), originally called the "Southern League." Founded in Alabama in 1994, the LOS swiftly became an influential leader of the neo-Confederate movement. While the SCV and the UDC were largely focused on history and heritage, the LOS sought to define southern identity based on its own interpretation of the past and to reverse what it regarded as the "emasculation of southern heritage."[15]

This new movement marked the beginning of the South's new civil religion and diverged from that of the Lost Cause, which had emerged immediately after the Civil War.[16] The narrative of honor and chivalry were still there, but neo-Confederates took a more politically active stance to defend southern heritage and its symbols. They spoke against ideas of "political correctness" and were unapologetic about the southern past as they interpreted it. Led by a group of male academics that included professors of history Michael Hill and Grady McWhiney, which the LOS referred to as its "brain trust," the group also took advantage of the emerging Internet to create an online following and to spread its message.

Like political conservatives who had co-opted the language of civil rights before them, the LOS and those who ascribed to its philosophy co-opted the language of multiculturalism as a means of both undermining multiculturalism and defending Confederate heritage. The term "Confederate American," for example, emerged in this decade in battles over Confederate monuments. Over the next several years, the LOS-led neo-Confederate movement pressured older, more traditional southern heritage organizations, especially the SCV, to take a more active role to defend flags and monuments. The result was that any attack on Confederate symbols became an attack on their southern ancestors and them personally. Furthermore, attacks on Robert E. Lee's character or symbols of the man whom they revered for his manliness was, by default, regarded as an attack on white masculinity. Eventually, this movement's attempt to throw off the yoke of white regional emasculation led to a more radical approach to "reassert manly control" through the types of violence later seen in Charlottesville.[17] This marked a stark contrast to the way members of the SCV generally responded to attacks on Confederate symbols, which was to blame the Ku Klux Klan. In a letter to the editor of the Nashville *Tennessean* titled "Confederate Heritage Bashing Is Never the Answer," for example, the leader of the SCV in Franklin wrote of the Klan, "This small group of warped people are the main reason I constantly have to defend my Southern heritage and my Confederate ancestors."[18]

The rise of the League of the South emerged in response to racial progress as well as to what the *Atlanta Constitution* described in 1993 as "The Symbol War." While the regional division of the NAACP continued its pressure to remove the battle flag from the Georgia state flag, the article emphasized the "raging" battles over all Confederate symbols "used to identify the region." As the Reverend Joseph Lowery of the Southern Christian Leadership Conference explained, "It isn't going away with the flag. Everything that relates to slavery—and the Confederacy represents slavery—is going to be controversial for years to come." In fact, it was already happening.[19]

Confederate monuments and markers were facing challenges as never before. In Tennessee, Memphians were "pressing the city to evict the remains of Gen. Nathan Bedford Forrest, a founder of the Ku Klux Klan," from the park created in his name, where a bronze statue of the general "is regularly vandalized." A black legislator in Louisiana climbed the Battle of Liberty Place obelisk in New Orleans, which celebrated the attempt in 1874 of the paramilitary White League to retake control of the state government and that contained explicitly white supremacist inscriptions, and "draped the shaft in blankets and sheets," vowing to return "and chain himself to the marker until it's destroyed." The obelisk had just been rededicated, and the *New Orleans Times-Picayune* referred to it as a "racial embarrassment." Additionally, an attempt by a Dallas, Texas, city councilman to have Robert E. Lee Park renamed led to a "raucous debate." Similar battles were being waged on Confederate symbols throughout the region.[20]

A new generation of African Americans were set on ridding the region of symbols tied to the defense of slavery. Many southern whites stiffened their resistance, fearing a domino effect that would lead to monument removal. In Georgia, Republican state representative Mark Burkhalter reassured the white constituents he represented in Alpharetta by proposing a bill to make defacing a monument punishable by up to seven years in prison. While that bill did not emerge from the rules committee, Georgia eventually passed a bill protecting Confederate monuments in 2019.[21] In response to the possibility of monument removal in his state, Charles Park of Rock Hill, South Carolina, founded a group called the "Confederate States of America Historical Preservation Society." According to Hill, "The attack on Confederate heritage is part of an overall Afrocentric scheme to get rid of white male European history."[22]

Efforts to find common ground were rare. In early 1990s Richmond, there was a desire among black city council members to add statues of civil rights heroes along Monument Avenue. As Councilman Henry Richardson reminded white city council members, "When blacks took over city government, we didn't go on an orgy of destruction tearing down Confederate things. In fact, we spent $500,000 improving monuments. We respected their heritage; now it's time for them to respect ours." One white city councilman pushed back, suggesting that placing a civil rights statue alongside the city's grand Confederate monuments was like "putting a toilet in your living room." Richardson ignored such offensive commentary, choosing instead to speak to the larger meaning of these statues so beloved by many white southerners. "We're not just talking about statues," he said. "We're talking about values and memory and the things we hold dear." And those values differed depending on one's racial perspective.[23]

In Memphis, the effort to create the National Civil Rights Museum was regarded as a means of achieving parity on the city's landscape. Memphis attorney D'Army Bailey, a member of the Tennessee Historical Commission who led the effort to establish the museum, bristled at the continued existence of the Nathan Bedford Forrest monument in the city, which he saw "as a political statement." Bailey understood that "it was put there as a statement of agreement and celebration of the man," and he confirmed his contempt for the racism it represented. "I always wished I'd had the courage to take a bucket of paint to that thing," he lamented.[24]

The *Atlanta Constitution* also asked historians to weigh in on the moment. John Boles, history professor at Rice University and editor of the *Journal of Southern History*, responded that "removing monuments and renaming streets doesn't change what happened," adding, "I don't think we should be sanitizing our history; we should be learning from it. These symbols are no cause for censorship or celebration, they're the cause for sober reflection." When asked about renaming schools, documentarian Ken Burns replied to a question about a school named for Confederates: "I'm not against all the Robert E. Lee Highs as long as we can get beyond the mythology and teach about ignorance." Writer Shelby Foote, a favorite among the southern heritage set, unsurprisingly opposed removing Confederate symbols. "I have black friends who are very offended by the Bedford Forrest monument here [in Memphis]. I can see their point of view, but I have some trouble with it." He justified his stance by saying, "Napoleon was ugly to women—does that mean they should remove all his statues in Europe?" The paper also quoted C. Vann Woodward, esteemed historian of the South. Woodward felt comfortable with changes to the Georgia state flag but did "not want to see a revisionist war on Confederate symbols." He didn't believe that one could deny the past "because a particular cause has become unpopular"; that would be "carrying fashion to the extreme." Notably, the paper did not ask either a woman or an African American historian to weigh in.[25] Common ground was hard enough to find, but the failure to even represent these voices made consensus impossible.

■ ■ ■

One way in which some cities sidestepped removing Confederate monuments was through the placement of what some today call "counter monuments"—in other words, monuments that countered the presence of Confederate monuments. While these represented well-intended efforts to reclaim public space for the African American community, the long-term effect was to make reckoning with Confederate monuments more difficult. In a few places, including in Greensboro and Charlotte in North Carolina, the addition of a bust or statue of Dr. Martin Luther King Jr. served that purpose.[26] In Richmond, the effort to place a statue of Arthur Ashe—the black tennis hero—among those of Confederates on Monument Avenue functioned as a counter monument and became the means by which African Americans sought to reclaim public space for their community. But what seemed like a simple solution—the addition of one monument to a native son—led to considerable debate among the city's black and white citizens and council members, once again laying bare the racial divide over the symbols of southern memory.

There had been no statue added to Monument Avenue since

1929, and in the early 1990s calls for monuments to civil rights heroes were abandoned in favor of erecting one to Ashe, the tennis great who had won both the U.S. Open and Wimbledon. Before his death from AIDS in 1993, he approved a design for the statue but not the site. Former Virginia governor Douglas Wilder, the nation's first elected black governor and a personal friend of Ashe, believed the Ashe statue belonged on Monument Avenue. Wilder referred to the monuments to Confederates as "heroes from another era which would deny the aspirations of Arthur Ashe." He believed that honoring Ashe along the same street as Lee and Jackson sent the message, "I, too, speak for Virginia."[27]

The Richmond City Council was ultimately responsible for the decision to add the Ashe statue to Monument Avenue. The Planning Commission gave its unanimous consent, and city manager Robert C. Bobb proclaimed that "no further government approval" was required, setting the groundbreaking for July 10, 1995, on what would have been the tennis star's fifty-second birthday. But as the *Boston Globe* reported, both black and white Richmonders "shared a mutual dismay." Many African Americans believed that the monument to Ashe belonged in a more appropriate location, far from Confederate statues, and several local whites expressed concern about the historic integrity of Monument Avenue. They wanted to be heard, and on June 26, the city council held a public discussion on the matter.[28]

In the week leading up to the city council's meeting, more than 400 people called city hall, 90 percent of whom opposed the location. R. Wayne Byrd, a thirty-eight-year-old heating technician, attended the meeting as a representative of an organization called the "Heritage Preservation Association." This title belied its real purpose, which was to promote the display of the Confederate battle flag. Byrd, his chest dripping with Confederate medals, lectured the black-majority city council. "If there's a hidden political agenda to put an Afro-American on Monument Avenue, they ought to honor the blacks who fought for the Confederacy," he said, promoting an ongoing myth about black military service to the South during the Civil War, for which there is no factual evidence. Like other southern whites, he spoke of Monument Avenue as "hallowed ground" and believed that adding the statue of

Ashe to the thoroughfare "[violated] the historic sensibilities of Richmond's Confederate American population." Henry Richardson, one of the five black council members, fired back that even though "Arthur didn't ride a horse, and didn't shoot a gun," he was still "a hero." During a break in the proceedings, Richardson told a reporter, "Everybody's dancing around the question, which is, 'Do we put a black man on Monument Avenue?'"[29]

The Richmond City Council decided to hold another hearing on July 17 to consider alternatives, and during the three-week interim, the furor only continued. White citizens left messages with the city clerk that included racial slurs, and when the day of the hearing arrived, 100 people signed up to speak. The meeting, which was televised, lasted seven hours. A black woman named Shirley Jackson, who wore what the *New York Times* described as "an African dress," proclaimed, "We call it Monument Avenue, not Confederate Avenue." Some white men wore "Rebel insignia," and during one heated moment a white male was ejected from the room for interrupting a woman labor relations consultant who suggested that all of the statues be razed. White city councilman Tim Kaine, who later rose through the ranks of his state's Democratic Party to become both governor and U.S. Senator, claimed his mind had been changed by the testimony he heard. "The symbolic considerations outweighed the practical considerations," he said, and he shifted his vote in favor of the Monument Avenue site.[30]

The hearing over adding the statue of Arthur Ashe to Monument Avenue ended at 1:00 a.m. with a unanimous vote by the city council of 7–0. Another year went by before the monument was unveiled, but on July 10, 1996, the twelve-foot bronze statue of the first black man to win Wimbledon was installed. The ceremony was met by protesters, but Douglas Wilder, the statue's most vociferous advocate, proclaimed that Monument Avenue was "now an avenue for all people."[31]

■ ■ ■

While the 1990s played out, monument building continued alongside a rising white nationalist movement. In 1998 Jack Kershaw, a staunch segregationist and amateur sculptor, and more famously known as the attorney for James Earl Ray, who murdered Dr.

Debating Removal in a Changing Political Landscape

Martin Luther King Jr., unveiled his monument to Nathan Bedford Forrest on private property just north of Brentwood, Tennessee, visible to passersby driving along Interstate 65. The statue of Forrest honored the former slave trader and Confederate general whose reputation for wartime brutality and postwar violence as the first Grand Wizard of the Ku Klux Klan made him a reviled figure. Kershaw defended his decision by telling a reporter, "Someone needs to say a good word for slavery." For someone like Kershaw, who was also a cofounder of the League of the South, the Confederate general offered a model of violent white supremacy he felt deserved a place of honor. And while neo-Confederates and anti-racists alike regarded the monument as the most hideous sculpture ever erected of a Confederate icon, its timing coincided with a revival of Forrest as a "virile hero."[32]

The Confederate general's resurgence in the 1990s had much to do with how he was portrayed by the author Shelby Foote, as well as with Ken Burns's use of Foote's interpretation of Forrest in his 1990 documentary on the Civil War. The film *Forrest Gump*, whose main character was named for Nathan Bedford Forrest, also helped to soften how Forrest was perceived. Yet it was Foote who did the most to restore the general's reputation. His 1952 book, *Shiloh*, painted an image of Forrest as the embodiment of heroic southern white masculinity, and Burns's popular documentary gave him an even larger platform. The idea of the war hero appealed to many of the region's white men, especially racial conservatives who had felt emasculated by the changing politics and demographics of the South since the 1960s.[33]

As the twenty-first century began, white citizens in Selma, Alabama, also decided that Nathan Bedford Forrest deserved to be honored in their town despite the fact that during the Battle of Selma on April 2, 1865, the town was surrendered to Union forces while General Forrest escaped. Still, the fact that he tried to defend their town was enough for members of the "Friends of Forrest" who wanted to honor the man. Eventually, they raised the necessary money for a bust of the general that would sit on top of a pedestal and be placed on city-owned property. The monument, which cost $21,000, was unveiled on October 7, 2000, and immediately became the source of negative attention and racial division.

Erecting a monument to Nathan Bedford Forrest in a town where Dr. Martin Luther King Jr. led three marches in 1965 to fight for voting and civil rights appeared intentionally dismissive of that history, even cynical. It seemed even more disrespectful given that the town had just elected a black mayor for the first time in its history—James Perkins Jr. But this was also a town that so revered Confederate general and Alabama klansman Edmund Pettus that it named a bridge for him—the same bridge and site of the brutal "Bloody Sunday" beatings of peaceful civil rights marchers on March 7, 1965. On the day the monument was unveiled, Joanne Bland, cofounder and director of the National Voting Rights Museum in Selma, complained, "This is just a slap in the face to us. Why would they put that where all our kids can see it every day?" Pat Godwin, the woman who organized the unveiling ceremony, bristled at the protesters who showed up and chanted, "Nate got to go!" "Those people who preach cultural tolerance don't practice it," Godwin said. She suggested protesters should "visit the library," where they would learn that Forrest didn't start the KKK; he was merely "asked to be the national leader of the fraternity," demonstrating her own lack of historical understanding. Her statement also reflected a fundamental dismissal of Selma's history of racial oppression and violence. "Racial harmony won't come to this town until we have cultural tolerance," she lectured.[34]

In the week that followed the unveiling and protest, Selma's new mayor learned that city funds had been used to fund the Forrest monument. The *Montgomery Advertiser* revealed that five white members of the former city government had appropriated $3,100 from their personal discretionary funds for the memorial. In addition to the $2,000 that previous mayor Joe Smitherman gave, individual city council members gave, too. Jean Martin, who donated $100, claimed she was embarrassed by the revelation because she thought she was giving money for a reception after the monument was unveiled. "Never would I give to Nathan Bedford Forrest," she said, as she sought to explain herself to Mayor Perkins.[35]

Selma's newly elected city council was, for the first time, a black-majority council. This, in addition to the election of the town's first black mayor, meant that decisions about the Confederate monument would be handled differently. And, indeed it was. At their November 13 meeting, Mayor Perkins presented the council with a copy of a letter addressed to the Friends of Forrest Monument Committee instructing the committee to "move the monument [from the city-owned Smitherman Building] no later than December 11, 2000 to any privately owned property of its choice, provided the site complies with city zoning ordinances." If the committee did not comply, the city would move it.[36] The monument had to go. But it was not going without a public fight.

Initially, the battle was fought in letters to the editor of the *Selma Times-Journal*. Most of the letter writers claimed that Forrest had been maligned by historians and that the monument simply represented a part of history. In what was becoming a regular occurrence of whites co-opting language for their cause, one person called those who wanted to have it removed "racists." However, it was Jimmy Poe, writing from Edgewood, New Mexico, who revealed the racist sentiments of monument defenders. In his letter to the editor, he called the men and women offended by the statue "knuckle-dragging crybabies." He referred to the mayor as an "idiot" and to those who supported the mayor's position as "his gang." Then he asked, "How many more misguided little towns across the South is this happening in?"[37]

As the date of the monument's impending removal approached, the Friends of Forrest, led by Pat Godwin, organized a parade where participants collectively "prayed in honor of the Confederate Civil War general" and had speeches about southern heritage. H. K Edgerton, a black man from North Carolina who famously donned a Confederate uniform and defended the battle flag and the Lost Cause throughout the South (something he continued to do as late as 2020), came to Selma and was photographed wearing a placard around his neck that read "Heritage Not Hate." Edgerton, an outlier among black southerners, spouted Lost Cause rhetoric about preserving history and also claimed that there needed to be a "tolerance of culture," by which he meant Confederate culture.[38]

Around 300 people attended the parade, which was publicized as the "Parade of Tolerance." Reverend Cecil Williamson, the pastor of the Crescent Hill Presbyterian Church who gave the keynote address at the monument's unveiling, also spoke at the rally that closed the parade. "We should never be ashamed of our heritage, but we should be ashamed of those who are," he said. Williamson spent a lot of his speech railing against critics of the monument for not tolerating those who were simply "honoring Southern culture," which in this context was decidedly white. Then, as happens at the end of a sermon in church when the collection plate is passed around, the Friends of Forrest asked the crowd for donations to help with legal expenses.

These efforts were all for naught. The city moved the monument to the Old Live Oak Cemetery inside of "Confederate Circle," among the graves of the Confederate dead, making it the first city in the nation to remove a Confederate monument from government-owned property.[39]

Still, even after the move, the continued existence of a monument to Nathan Bedford Forrest in the city limits of Selma remained a "slap in the face" for many black residents. Over the next several years, people tossed garbage on the monument, and someone once tied a rope around the bust in an attempt to rip it down but failed. Then, in 2012, someone succeeded in stealing the bronze bust of Forrest from the pedestal where it was affixed. Benny Austin, spokesman for the Friends of Forrest, called on "all persons to stand against any attacks on our common history, its monuments and memorials." The group, along with the SCV and private donors, raised enough money to offer a $20,000 reward for information that would allow them to recover the bust, which cost just $9,000 when it was cast. But the bust was never recovered. Instead, the money went toward the creation of a facsimile from the original sculptor, who resided in Maine.

The reinstallation of the bust sparked a new round of conflict. Later in 2012, Pat Godwin announced plans to give Confederate Circle a "new look" and to protect the new monument, which included security cameras. However, as construction began, several protesters laid down in the path of the cement truck to prevent it from doing the work. Malika Sanders-Fortier, daughter of local attorney and radio host Rose Sanders, created an online petition asking the city council to ban the monument and told a reporter, "Here we are on the 150th anniversary of the Civil War, and we're still having the same fights." Her mother concurred, saying, "For

Selma, of all places, to have a big monument to a Klansman is totally unacceptable." In the end, the new bust was erected, but the grand plans Godwin announced did not pan out. It revealed, once again, that the discourse on the meaning of Confederate monuments was as segregated as Selma still was in 2012.[40]

■ ■ ■

Southern universities were also dealing with the same issues and dynamics that Confederate monuments represented in the region's towns and cities. Yet public universities were bound by a different set of conventions. First, they were answerable to their diverse communities of students, faculty, workers, and administrators. They also benefited from public financial support through tuition and tax dollars. These conditions inevitably pushed difficult conversations around Confederate monuments front and center.

Around the same time that Selma's black residents sought to combat the presence of a monument to a known Klansman, the University of Louisville (UL) in Kentucky was engaged in a years-long effort to counter the Confederate monument sitting adjacent to its campus. It hadn't always been close to student foot traffic. But as the university grew in size, the seventy-five-foot monument, placed in 1895, became entirely surrounded by the campus. In 2002 a group of UL faculty organized to advocate for a plan to reenvision the small triangle of ground on which the monument sat. They wanted to bring balance to the memorial by creating "Freedom Park," which would leave the monument untouched but would add "a statue or plaza focused on global struggles for freedom." And on November 25, 2002, the UL Board of Trustees approved the proposal for its creation.[41]

The Freedom Park Task Force, created in 2003, was cochaired by Dr. J. Blaine Hudson, professor and chair of the Pan-African Studies department. Hudson had been part of the UL community since the 1960s, when he had been a student leader of the Black Student Union. The other cochair was Mitchell Payne, then the acting vice president for business affairs at UL. The task force's goals included an interactive space of exhibits, such as one on the Underground Railroad so central to Louisville's history, as well as a "plaza devoted to struggles for freedom." On January 20, 2003,

UL president James Ramsey dedicated Freedom Park and pledged the university's commitment to develop a "balanced and accurate interpretation" of history on the site.[42]

Progress on the park was achingly slow, and soon enough there were calls for a reconsideration of the plan. In 2005, Reverend Louis Coleman, executive director of the Justice Resource Center in Louisville, called on local government to remove the Confederate monument. "A statue of this nature does not belong in the middle of a roadway that connects to a college that boasts [its] diversity," he said. Hudson, who was still heavily involved in the creation of Freedom Park, assured the community that a sculptor had been hired to create something to counter the memorial; he hoped that the park would be completed in two to three years. Coleman was more emphatic that the monument needed to go. "Our kids shouldn't have to walk past that every day when they're going to their classes," he said. He also suggested, as many more would after the Charlottesville uprising, that the monument should go to a history museum.[43]

The mere suggestion of removal set off a firestorm of letters to the editor of the *Louisville Courier-Journal*. On February 28, 2005, the newspaper published those from monument defenders. Their letters not only demonstrated a strict adherence to Lost Cause arguments about states' rights and heritage but also attacked Coleman, and their criticism over possible removal came out as thinly veiled racism. William Hayes of Louisville wrote that the Justice Resource Center's proposal to remove the monument was "preposterous," and he advised Coleman that if he wanted "to do something about eliminating slavery, [his organization] should take a look at what is enslaving blacks in Louisville today. . . . It is certainly not the Confederate Monument," Hayes continued, "but drug use, black-on-black violence, and a breakdown in the traditional black family," a sentiment that echoed what whites in Shreveport had expressed in their local paper in the late 1980s. He went on to preach to Coleman that he should focus on issues "that have meaning for our black citizens today." His use of "our black citizens" in 2005 was strikingly similar to the phrase "our negroes" used by southern white supremacists a century earlier. Mark Roth of Louisville joined the chorus of defenders by providing a Lost Cause interpretation of the Civil War as nothing more than an issue of states' rights. Another man wrote to say he feared that "these activists want to create an American Europe" (likely a euphemism for socialism), and he was tired of listening to all of this dialogue about "diversity."[44]

One week after the monument defenders had their say, the *Courier-Journal* published a completely different set of letters. Ivonne Rovira defended Coleman and suggested that the person who wrote that Coleman should know more history ought to take his own advice. "Stop the old canard that the Civil War was about states' rights. Anyone who holds [that] states' rights was anything but an after-the-fact justification for keeping black folks in their place is the one who doesn't know history," she said. John Baker asked, in reference to the monument, "Is the public commemoration of the institution of slavery justified? I believe only the most ardent supporters of the archaic mindset this statue represents would answer yes." He ended his letter by calling on citizens to "come together [and] get on the people's train and remove this abhorrent memorial." Mattie Jones of the Justice Resource Center also weighed in with a letter whose sentiments had been shared by black southerners for more than a century. "The statue of the Confederate soldier speaks to me of honoring racism and hatred that African Americans have suffered and are continuing to suffer," she said.[45]

Freedom Park eventually opened in 2012, and as had been Dr. J. Blaine Hudson's vision, the park contained sculptures and exhibits that provided a more complete account of Louisville's history, including the city's African American history since the eighteenth century. The Confederate monument remained intact, while the park offered some counterbalance to the message it represented to black citizens. Nonetheless, it did not erase how black citizens felt about the monument and its message of racism —and the monument's days were numbered. In November 2016, it would finally be removed.[46]

■ ■ ■

For most of the twentieth century, moving a monument was not an uncommon act. Many Confederate statues were placed well before the mass production of automobiles. Horses and wagons might have avoided run-ins with Johnny Reb on his pedestal, but as southern cities and towns built roads, monuments simply got in the way. At the same time, new statues continued to be added to the regional landscape. "The Confederate monument was naked for almost a century," an article in the *News Leader* of Staunton, Virginia, began in 2007. The reference was to an empty pedestal that had been erected by the UDC in the city of Norfolk in 1912 but moved in 1987 to Elmwood Cemetery to make way for road construction. Thus, the Norfolk pedestal went into the cemetery where, in 2007, it finally got its Confederate soldier—hewn from granite sourced from a quarry in China.[47]

The Norfolk monument represents one of thirty-five new monuments built since 2000. Several others have been rededicated after preservation efforts, because the aging stone had taken a beating by the weather.[48] In Mississippi in 2009, both a proposal to place a new monument to Jefferson Davis on the grounds of the state capitol and an effort to preserve an old monument to Davis illustrate the state's continued dedication to the Lost Cause and a native son—the first and only president of the Confederacy.

In 2008, the Sons of Confederate Veterans commissioned a life-size bronze statue of Jefferson Davis holding the hands of two little boys. One was his son Joe Davis, while the other was of a biracial boy named Jim Limber, who the Sons claimed "had been adopted by the Davis family." The story of Jim Limber is a complicated one and, like much of the Lost Cause, contains mythical elements. In 1864 in Richmond, he was taken in by Davis's wife, Varina, when she allegedly saw him being abused by his caretaker, a black woman. Limber was around the same age as Joe and lived with the Davises in the Confederate White House. There is no legal evidence that Limber was adopted, just stories from Varina's diary in which she refers to him as a family "pet." Regardless, the SCV sought to situate the former Confederate president into a story of paternalism that would be represented by the statue.[49]

This new Jefferson Davis statue, which cost the SCV $100,000, had been orphaned since the Sons commissioned it. They first tried to place it with what is now the American Civil War Museum in Richmond and failed. So, they returned to Davis's home state. A bill began its way through the Mississippi statehouse to accept the new statue of Davis, but it never passed. Representative George Flaggs, an African American Democrat from Vicksburg, said that the bill for the SCV statue "was offensive to a lot of lawmakers." In the end, the legislature decided to pass a completely different bill, directing the Mississippi Division of Archives and History to restore the Davis statue near the Old Capitol Museum in downtown Jackson, originally unveiled in 1891—which it did to the tune of $95,000.[50] And in 2009, the SCV statue also found a home in Mississippi, at Beauvoir, the last home of Davis, located in Biloxi, which is maintained by the Mississippi Division of the SCV with generous funding from the state legislature.[51]

The story of what happened in Mississippi illustrates both a financial and political commitment to Confederate monuments in the state. In total, the two Davis monuments represented an investment of nearly $200,000—still a substantial sum in the twenty-first century. But it was the political involvement by state politicians, not just a local city council, that suggests that paying fealty to these symbols, which was becoming increasingly common, played well with Republican constituents, and the issue could be deployed by those running for office. At the same time, for politicians in states whose loyalties were divided between parties, or those with national ambition, support for Confederate symbols sometimes proved problematic.

In the 2006 election for governor of Florida, Republican candidate Charlie Crist chose state representative Jeff Kottkamp from Cape Coral to be his running mate for lieutenant governor. Kottkamp's record in the state legislature came under closer scrutiny, and before he made his first appearance with Crist, he found himself defending a bill he had cosponsored to keep the Confederate flag flying over the state capitol in Tallahassee. The bill was filed in response to the action taken by Governor Jeb Bush to remove the flag from capitol grounds in 2001, which he had done in an effort to avoid the same controversy that had happened in South Carolina, where there'd been a years-long NAACP boycott. Of the forty cosponsors of Kottkamp's legislation, seven were Democrats, two were African Americans, and one of them was the incoming House Speaker, Marco Rubio.[52]

Kottkamp, originally from Indiana, angered black lawmakers

with his bill, and the issue continued to dog him on the campaign trail. In an effort to defend himself, he told reporters, "I don't ever remember the flag being mentioned." He continued, "I think it was primarily to preserve historical monuments, like Confederate monuments and World War I monuments." The bill, like those passed after 2015, proposed to block local governments from permanently removing or relocating any historical monument from public property and included "historic flags." The 2006 bill did not pass, but it offered a model for future monument legislation adopted across the South that included language about protecting "monuments that commemorate any war in which the United States participated" when in fact the intent was to protect Confederate monuments.[53]

Kottkamp survived his trial by fire, as both he and Crist were ushered into office in November 2006, but a few years later the spotlight was on Texas governor Rick Perry. In 2011, Perry, who was already being considered as a possible contender for the Republican presidential nomination, came under scrutiny for his stance on Confederate symbols while lieutenant governor. Years earlier, in 2000, which saw an NAACP victory in South Carolina, where the flag was removed from the capitol dome, and pressure on Georgia to change its state flag, the civil rights organization asked Texas to remove bronze plaques containing images of the Confederate battle flag from the entryway to the state supreme court and the court of appeals.[54]

Rick Perry's response was to cozy up to the SCV. In a private letter to the Sons in Texas, he wrote, "I want you to know that I oppose efforts to remove Confederate monuments, plaques, and memorials from public property." At the same time, he advocated for local control by saying, "Communities should decide whether statues or other memorials are appropriate for their community." Publicly, he argued that the plaques at issue should remain and that Texans "should never forget our history." In the years since 2000, and after he was elected governor, Perry consistently defended Confederate symbols, because as one reporter noted, "Confederate symbols and Southern institutions can still be good politics below the Mason-Dixon line." But as he eyed a run for president, his Confederate sympathies did not ultimately play well outside of the region, at least in 2011 when he announced his bid for the nomination.[55]

While political opportunism over the issue of Confederate monuments was mostly contained in the South as the second decade of the twenty-first century began, it came roaring to the national stage in 2015. There seemed to no longer be a need, or a desire, to hide from a record of defending Confederate symbols, even in the aftermath of the murder of nine black parishioners by a young white nationalist. Moreover, the gutting of the Voting Rights Act in 2013, which led to egregious acts of voter suppression, meant that once again African Americans were being cut out of the democratic process that provided a path to removing Confederate monuments through civic action. The symbols of their ancestors' enslavement, of white supremacy, and of racial oppression continued to haunt the southern landscape.

CODA

Since 2000 we have witnessed the growth of electronic communities, first through websites and blogs and then through the creation of Facebook in 2004 and Twitter in 2006. For most Americans in the early days of social media, these outlets provided opportunities to stay in touch with friends and family, to follow a celebrity, or to catch up on news. While this remains true, it is also true that the Internet and social media have been used for more nefarious purposes—to spread hate, white supremacist ideology, and the causes of white nationalism.

The League of the South was quick to take advantage of these new forms of communication to promote the neo-Confederate cause, particularly its goal of creating a separate and hierarchical Christian ethno-state. In fact, I discovered what was then known as the Southern League while a doctoral student writing about the United Daughters of the Confederacy. I sent an email through the website to learn more about this new organization. A man from Texas, known as the site's "Rebmaster," responded. He explained the league's goals, which included seceding from the United States to form a separate southern nation led by white men. As I continued to ask questions in our exchange, he soon went quiet and questioned whether I might be an "agent provocateur."

In the time since, I've watched as the organization evolved and new ones were created, some more violent than others but all dedicated to a new southern nationalism or white nationalism in which Confederate symbols—both flags and monuments—are sacrosanct. And just as the politics of the South has influenced our national politics, the ideas and beliefs of southern nationalism have influenced white nationalism. This cadre of white supremacist groups, many of which were organized outside of the South, converged in Charlottesville, Virginia, in 2017. Their stated purpose? To protect the Confederate monument of Robert E. Lee from removal. The reality of what was known as the Unite the Right rally was far more sinister. And their simmering hatred was not isolated. It had emerged two years earlier in an act of mass murder in Charleston, South Carolina.

6

CHARLESTON, CHARLOTTESVILLE, AND CONTINUED CHALLENGES TO REMOVAL

On June 17, 2015, Charleston, South Carolina, was blazing hot. With the temperature hovering close to 100 degrees, even the most ardent tourists sought shelter in air-conditioned shops and restaurants. Locals went about their routines, and for dedicated churchgoers, the evening was reserved for midweek Bible study and prayer meetings. This is what members of Emanuel African Methodist Episcopal (AME) Church were doing when a young white man walked in and joined them. Dressed in a sweatshirt and dark pants that immediately stuck out as unusual given the summer heat, he took a seat next to Reverend Clementa Pinckney, the forty-one-year-old pastor. He sat there for an hour before he drew a gun and opened fire on the men and women who had welcomed him. As he did, he yelled at them, "You rape our

women and you're taking over our country. And you have to go."
He then coolly walked out, got in his black Hyundai sedan, and
drove away.[1]

Throughout the evening the news of mass murder inside a
historically black church swept across the United States. The following day, a pall hung over Charleston as locals walked in silence, dazed by what occurred. Nine people had been murdered in
"Mother Emanuel," one of the oldest African American churches
in the country and the oldest AME church in the South. The iconic
structure had been built in 1891, but its history dated to 1817, just
a few years before cofounder Denmark Vesey had led a slave rebellion in 1822. Almost two centuries later, the church's history
was now marred by a racist act that took precious lives: those of
Reverend Pinckney, Tywanza Sanders, Cynthia Hurd, DePayne
Middleton-Doctor, Sharonda Coleman-Singleton, Susie Jackson,
Ethel Lee Lance, Daniel Simmons, and Myra Thompson.

The young man who entered Mother Emanuel was twenty-
one-year-old Dylann Roof of Lexington, South Carolina, a town
located near the state capital of Columbia. He had been identified
by an older sister who notified authorities when she saw the cam-
era footage of him entering the church. The following morning a
woman in Gastonia, North Carolina, alerted authorities after rec-
ognizing Roof by his slight build and bowl-shaped haircut. Police then followed his car along Interstate 85 and into the town
of Shelby, the birthplace of author Thomas Dixon, whose racist
books, including *The Clansman* (1905), played no small part in the
rise of the second Ku Klux Klan. It was there that officers appre-
hended Roof during a traffic stop. In the hours that followed, the
news media scrambled to find answers that might help explain his
murderous rampage. What they discovered drew Americans into
national and political discussions over the meaning and existence
of Confederate symbols so prevalent across the South. It began
with the battle flag, but soon monuments came into sharp focus.[2]

The tragedy in Charleston kicked off a new phase in the long
history of Confederate symbols, but especially Confederate monuments. Even before the massacre of the Emanuel Nine, monuments had become symbols of the country's political divide and
another subject in the stable of issues conservative politicians

employed to stoke a culture war. Since June 2015, debates over Confederate monuments have come to symbolize competing visions not only of the South but also of the nation. And throughout the region where conservative politicians held power, those politicians instituted laws that thwarted efforts at removal. The absence of legal channels for removal or any democratic recourse for changing the monumental landscape gave rise to grassroots protests, while the push to protect monuments at all costs actually led to their being vandalized and ripped from their pedestals.

■ ■ ■

Journalists' efforts to unearth explanations for Roof's act of mass murder exposed the region's strong ties to the Confederate tradition and the historical actors who raised and defended monuments to the Confederacy. Details also revealed that in the course of his young life, Dylann Roof went seeking, and found, websites that supported his beliefs about race. Influenced by sites that promoted white supremacist ideology, including that of the Council of Conservative Citizens—an even more racist reboot of the White Citizens' Councils of the 1950s and 1960s—Roof found the justification he needed to enter Emanuel AME to commit mass murder. He viewed videos of black-on-white violence posted online, which fueled his anger and led to his determination that "someone needed to do something about it for the white race." His interest in Confederate history led him to visit the South Carolina Confederate Museum, and on his personal website, he posted a photograph of himself with the Confederate battle flag. That photo of Roof in shorts, peering over sunglasses perched on the end of his nose, with a handgun in one hand and the battle flag resting across his left shoulder, went viral. Almost immediately, there were calls to remove the Confederate flag from the state capitol.[3]

It wasn't the first time South Carolina's Confederate battle flag had faced challenges. The NAACP had campaigned for years to have it removed from the capitol dome, citing it as a painful reminder of slavery, segregation, and racial violence. Its efforts succeeded in 2000, but not without a compromise to appease white conservatives in the state legislature. While the state removed the flag from the dome, it was guaranteed a place on capitol grounds, high on a flagpole adjacent to the Confederate monument, where

In the days following the murder of nine parishioners at
Emanuel AME Church in Charleston, South Carolina, on June 17, 2015,
pressure to remove the Confederate battle flag from the grounds of
the state capitol in Columbia intensified and resulted in protests and
counterprotests around the Confederate monument.
(AP Photo/Rainier Ehrhardt)

it remained in the immediate aftermath of the Charleston massacre. And because election year politics were already in full swing by the summer of 2015, the battle flag became a focus of national public debates in the context of what the *New York Times* referred to as the country's increasing "anguish about race."[4]

Republican candidates for president faced pressure to respond to questions about how the tragedy exposed America's problem with race. South Carolina's senator Lindsey Graham, a presidential contender, called Dylann Roof a "racial jihadist," deflecting from the real issues of domestic terrorism and the influence of white supremacist ideology in his own state. When it came to the question of removing the Confederate flag from capitol grounds, former Florida governor Jeb Bush said he believed Governor Nikki Haley would "do right" by South Carolina. As governor, Bush himself had ordered the flag removed from the grounds of the Florida State Capitol in 2001. Senator Marco Rubio, also of Florida, agreed stating that he believed Haley would "make the right choice," though neither he nor Jeb Bush was willing to commit to saying it should be removed. Candidate Donald Trump said he thought it should be removed and put in a museum, while Wisconsin's governor, Scott Walker, remained mum on the issue. Most Republican candidates eventually conceded that Roof's act was based in racial hatred but punted when asked if the flag should be removed. All trod lightly for fear of upsetting the GOP's conservative base in the South, where Confederate symbols were revered.[5]

Yet it was not just the Confederate flag that saturated the southern landscape with representations of the region's ties to racism and white supremacy. Southerners of all races lived on streets named for Confederate soldiers, attended schools named for Confederate heroes like Robert E. Lee and Stonewall Jackson, and were confronted by Confederate monuments on the grounds of courthouses and state capitols. As Bryan Stevenson of the Equal Justice Initiative explained, "The landscape is littered with monuments that talk proudly about the Confederacy and leave no record about the lynchings of the era," many of which took place on those same courthouse lawns.[6]

For the time being, the battle flag was the most pressing issue, and five days after the murders in Charleston, Governor Nikki Haley called for the flag to be removed from capitol grounds. She had not previously supported removal, but such a high-profile murder of nine African Americans could not be ignored. "We are not going to allow this symbol to divide us any longer," she said. Cornell Brooks, national president of the NAACP, also pushed for removal. "Bringing down that flag will not bring about an end to racial hatred," he said, "but it would do a lot to prevent the nurturing of this kind of hatred." Nevertheless, the South Carolina General Assembly, dominated by a Republican majority in both chambers, debated the issue for days as some sought options to keep the flag flying. Their sluggishness left open a window for those who wanted the flag removed immediately and sought to remedy the situation through direct action.[7]

Early on June 27, a Saturday, two young activists, Bree Newsome and James Tyson, both thirty, traveled from North Carolina to the South Carolina State Capitol in Columbia. Using climbing gear, Newsome was already halfway up the flagpole before she was noticed by capitol police and ordered to come down. She ignored the command and continued her climb, unhooking the flag and removing it before descending and facing arrest. Significantly, the two were charged with defacing a monument, which under South Carolina's Heritage Protection Act included the Confederate battle flag. In a statement emailed to news media, Newsome wrote, "We removed the flag today because we can't wait any longer. . . . We are sincere about dismantling white supremacy and building toward true racial justice and equality."[8] The dramatic photo of Newsome descending the flagpole with the Confederate battle flag in hand went viral and has since become an iconic image of resistance to the banner once carried by Confederate armies in a war to perpetuate slavery.

But though Newsome and Tyson's direct action forced the issue, it did not quite resolve it. Within the hour, a new battle flag replaced the one Newsome had removed, and by ten o'clock that morning several cars and trucks arrived flying Confederate flags and circled the statehouse. These flag supporters rallied on state grounds around the base of the Confederate monument, a common tactic by neo-Confederates seeking to make a collective statement in defense of racist symbols, proving that Dylann Roof was no outlier and the ideology he subscribed to was widely shared.[9]

To put the issue to rest, the South Carolina General Assembly still had to pass a bill. After intense debates about what it meant to permanently remove the flag, which had been there since 1962, they finally did so. Governor Haley signed the bill into law on July 9, and the flag came down for good two days later. In that moment, South Carolinians of all races gathered near the flag as it was being removed, many of them standing adjacent to the Confederate monument that towered over the crowd, where they took photos to mark this historic moment. For some the flag's removal stung, while others celebrated it as a sign of healing and victory. The *New York Times* asserted that the flag's removal "will serve as dramatic notice that many of the Confederate signs and symbols that have long dotted the Southern landscape may now be vulnerable to revision and removal."[10]

Among those who attended South Carolina's flag removal were a few who believed the vulnerability of Confederate monuments was cause for greater alarm. One young man predicted, "They're going to want to take down the Confederate monument," adding, "Everybody wants to be a victim." Members of the KKK announced they would hold a rally in Columbia, and Sons of Confederate Veterans spokesman Charles Kelly Barrow issued a statement calling the flag's removal "a wave of cultural cleansing" that "sullies" the names of Confederate ancestors. Places like New Orleans, Tampa, and Austin were already discussing taking down flags and removing monuments, and monument defenders across the South were worried about what might come next.

A movement was already afoot to remove the statue of Nathan Bedford Forrest in Memphis, Tennessee. Days before the flag came down in Columbia, the Memphis City Council voted unanimously to begin the process of removing the statue and the remains of Forrest and his wife, encased in the monument's marble base since 1905. Forrest was particularly offensive in a black-majority city like Memphis, which had already scrubbed his name from a park in 2013. Nick Hicks, a twenty-six-year-old black Memphian, said he saw "terrorism, racism, and white supremacy" when he looked at the Forrest statue, while Lee Millar, the sixty-five-year-old spokesman for the SCV, said it represented nothing more than "honor and valor." Forrest, he said, was "a great community man. He was an inspiration for everyone." The racial and generational divide over the statue was unmistakable and characteristic of the form these debates took in the aftermath of Charleston.[11]

To rally monument defenders, Millar organized a "birthday ceremony for Forrest," where attendees carried battle flags and wore T-shirts that read "Confederate Lives Matter." This was the third generation of neo-Confederates to co-opt the language of movements meant to draw attention to racial inequity. During the immediate post–civil rights era, whites had demanded "equality" for Confederate heritage. And in the middle of a movement pushing for multiculturalism, they proclaimed themselves "Confederate Americans." Seeing that the Black Lives Matter movement had been gaining momentum since its launch in 2014, they now declared "Confederate Lives Matter." In each instance, this tactic of co-opting language purposefully demeaned and diminished the original movements in hopes of returning the focus to white lives and white power structures.[12]

Memphis mayor A. C. Wharton Jr. responded to critics who claimed that removing monuments changed history by asking a more important question. "We can't unring a rung bell," he said about history as it related to the monument, "but how long do we have to pay fealty to it? That's what the monument represents. I'm resolved we are going to remove it." City councilman Myron Lowery also made a critical point about the reality of protesting monuments under Jim Crow, saying that if he had been alive in 1905 when the Forrest statue was unveiled and had tried to oppose it, "I could have been lynched." It's not as if Lowery or other black southerners had never wanted to publicly protest Confederate monuments in their communities. Rather, the threat of violence and their status as second-class citizens had long prevented them from doing so.[13]

The Memphis resolution passed, but it faced one more hurdle—the Tennessee Historical Commission. In 2013, the state legislature passed the Tennessee Heritage Protection Act that protected any and all war monuments, including those to the "War between the States," the Lost Cause term for the Civil War. It prohibited local governments from "removing, renaming, [or] relocating" monuments without first seeking a waiver from the Tennessee Historical Commission, but it did not issue any guidelines on how to do so. In truth, the politically appointed members were unlikely to grant permission. The City of Memphis had tried this route to remove the Forrest monument and was denied. Matters would remain stalled until December 2017—and in the meantime, this tactic would gain steam elsewhere, as GOP-dominated southern legislatures responded to the Charleston tragedy by doubling down to protect monuments.[14]

They had plenty of precedents to build on. South Carolina's Heritage Protection Act, passed in 2000, required a two-thirds supermajority in order to remove "any monument, marker, memorial, school, or street erected or named in honor of the Confederacy or the civil rights movement located on municipal, county, or state property." Tossing in "civil rights movement" was a cynical move given that the goal—after the NAACP boycott of South Carolina had led to the removal of the Confederate battle flag from the capitol dome that year—was to protect Confederate symbols. Virginia's law protecting monuments, passed in 1904, already made it illegal to "disturb or interfere with any monuments or memorials," and in 2016 a Republican-sponsored bill tried to strengthen the law but was vetoed by Governor Terry McAuliffe. Nonetheless, the old law remained in place as a deterrent to monument removal.[15]

All the while, new bills were being passed by Republican-dominated legislatures and signed into law by governors, and none was more poorly timed and racially insensitive than the one in North Carolina. Just one month after the Charleston massacre, on July 21, the House passed a bill that banned state agencies and local governments from taking down any "object of remembrance" on public property that "commemorates an event, a person, or military service that is part of North Carolina's history." The North Carolina law went further in prohibiting the moving of a monument to a museum or cemetery where historical context was possible. The law's official title, the "Cultural History Artifact Management and Patriotism Act," essentially served to preempt local authorities from removing Confederate monuments or even altering them with historical context without the approval of the North Carolina Historical Commission. Although Governor Pat McCrory had reservations about the provisions that prevented local governments from acting in the interests of their own communities, calling it "overreach into local decision making," he still signed the bill into law.[16]

As state representatives acted quickly to undercut local control through new monument laws, at least one southern politician was just as swift in pushing back. One week after the Charleston massacre, New Orleans mayor Mitch Landrieu called for the removal of monuments in his city, including those to Robert E. Lee, Jefferson Davis, and P. G. T. Beauregard and the obelisk honoring the Battle of Liberty Place, which David Duke once referred to as a "symbol of white power." While the Charleston tragedy moved Landrieu to make a public statement, he also claimed to have come to the decision a year earlier after discussions with his friend Wynton Marsalis, a jazz ambassador and New Orleans native. Six months to the day of the Charleston massacre, on December 17, the city council voted to remove all four of the city's Confederate monuments, which the *New York Times* called "one of the most sweeping gestures yet by an American city to sever ties with its Confederate past."[17]

Almost immediately, lawsuits were filed, legislators sought ways to prevent the city from removing monuments, and Governor Bobby Jindal claimed to be reviewing the state's Heritage Act to intervene. The city had used a local ordinance that allowed for the removal of monuments on public land if they became a "nuisance." In this case, they argued that monuments fostered ideas of white supremacy and might be used as "rallying points for violent demonstrations." The path to removal became bogged down in lawsuits, including one from the so-called Monumental Task Committee, whose attorney filed an injunction against removal. Eventually, however, the U.S. Fifth Circuit Court of Appeals unanimously held that the City of New Orleans could not be prevented from removing monuments on property it owned. On May 19, 2017, New Orleans began taking down the grand monument to Robert E. Lee, originally unveiled in 1884, and claimed to be the first city to remove a monument for the purpose of racial healing. While Selma, Alabama, actually already held that honor, the media attention given to the action in New Orleans proved far more significant to the national conversation about the role Confederate monuments had played in the South, especially in the aftermath of the Charleston massacre.

As the Lee statue was being removed, across town in Gallier Hall Mayor Landrieu delivered a much-heralded speech about the necessity of removing Confederate monuments in New Orleans.

Invited guests included Keith Plessy, a descendant of Homer Plessy, the plaintiff in the Supreme Court case that challenged segregation; descendants of slaves once owned by Georgetown University; and Claude Reese, a Freedom Rider from New Orleans. Landrieu's address began by invoking the city's history, which he referred to as "our history," and not in the way neo-Confederates used the term. Rather, Landrieu included the full complexity of people, racially and ethnically diverse, who made New Orleans a "city of many nations." He spoke of confronting the city's history, including its role in the slave trade and its slave markets. He called out the racial violence of lynching and of the beatings Freedom Riders endured. Then he directed his attention to the "self-appointed defenders of history and monuments" who conveniently relied on memories of omission. He rightly called the city's Confederate statuary "monuments to the Lost Cause" and declared their removal important to "healing and understanding each other."[18]

An important element of Mayor Landrieu's speech was his critique of what these monuments stood for, demonstrating an engagement with the historical record and the work of historians. "They're not just innocent remembrances of a benign history," he said. "These monuments celebrate a fictional, sanitized Confederacy: ignoring the death, ignoring enslavement, ignoring the terror that it actually stood for." Monuments, in essence, promoted a "false narrative." In his closing comments, he called on New Orleans's citizens to embrace the full 300-year history of the city, and not just the four years of the Confederacy.[19]

Landrieu's speech went viral, but for all the praise it received from historians and pundits across the country, the mayors of other cities that were home to Confederate monuments did not follow his example. If anything, southern states continued on their path of protecting these statues. Tennessee tightened its legislation in 2016 to resemble that of South Carolina—requiring a two-thirds majority in each house of the General Assembly to change the law. And, just two months prior to Mayor Landrieu's speech, in March 2017, the Alabama Memorial Preservation Act passed. Like the North Carolina law, the act prohibited "the relocation, removal, alteration, renaming, or disturbance of monuments located on public property." Monuments were defined as "a statue, portrait, or marker" on public property owned or leased by the state or the "county, municipal, or metropolitan government in the state." Permission to remove a monument had to be granted by the Committee on Alabama Monument Protection, which was a legislative committee filled by representatives unlikely to grant such approval. Moreover, if the state's attorney general determined that a city removed a monument without permission, it would be assessed a $25,000 fine for each violation.[20] Essentially, the act was intended to preempt local control.

This is where the issue of Confederate monuments stood in the spring of 2017: local governments continued to press for monument removal, even in states where laws prohibited it. One of the cities where the subject of removal had been festering since the Charleston massacre was Charlottesville, Virginia, and in August 2017, tensions would boil over as never before.

■ ■ ■

Charlottesville, home to the University of Virginia and Thomas Jefferson's Monticello, is also the site of monuments to Confederate generals Robert E. Lee and Stonewall Jackson, which had long been a source of irritation for the city's black citizens. And in the months following the Charleston massacre, as had happened to Confederate monuments in cities throughout the South, the Lee monument was targeted by protesters who painted the pedestal with the phrase "Black Lives Matter." In July 2017, someone splashed the statue with red paint. The latter act of vandalism was likely an expression of frustration with the slow pace of removal, which was hindered by Virginia's law protecting monuments. For its part, the five-member Charlottesville City Council had already voted 3–2 to remove the Lee statue and had renamed Lee Park "Emancipation Park," but in May 2017, following a lawsuit filed by a group called the Monument Fund, Inc., joined by members of the SCV and descendants of the sculptor, a judge issued an injunction that prevented removal for at least six months.[21]

The move to rename Lee Park and the prospect of removing the Lee statue struck members of white nationalist groups as an "erasure" of white heritage, and on Saturday, May 13, 2017, far right white nationalist leader Richard Spencer organized afternoon and evening demonstrations around the Lee monument. The thirty-nine-year-old Spencer, who coined the term "alt-right," led a large group of protesters who carried torches and chanted, "You will not replace us!" The short-lived demonstration lasted just ten minutes before counterprotesters and the Charlottesville City Police arrived, after which the crowd quickly dispersed. Yet it was a sign that the movement for monument removal would be met with resistance and foreshadowed events just three months later.[22]

White nationalists targeted Charlottesville a second time on August 12, 2017, again under the pretense of defending the monument from removal. Yet on the evening of August 11, before the scheduled noon protest at the Lee statue the following day, a column of around 250 young white men, mostly in their twenties and thirties and dressed in khaki pants and white polo shirts, marched through the University of Virginia campus carrying lighted tiki torches and chanting "Blood and Soil!," "You will not replace us!," and "Jews will not replace us!" The news media, tipped off by Richard Spencer, who coordinated the demonstration with Charlottesville resident Jason Kessler, arrived on campus around 9:00 p.m., just in time to capture the torchlit procession and participants' confrontation with a diverse group of around thirty university students who had locked arms around the base of the statue of Thomas Jefferson in front of the Rotunda. There, the torch-bearing white nationalists circled the students and, according to a report in the *Washington Post*, "made monkey noises at the black counterprotesters," as well as chanted "White lives matter!" According to press accounts, there was no law enforcement along the march, and it took several minutes before the police arrived and intervened.[23]

The nighttime procession of white nationalists paled in comparison to events the following day, as hundreds more white supremacists, along with neo-Nazis and Ku Klux Klan members, began arriving well in advance of the scheduled noontime gathering. They carried nationalist banners, shields, and clubs. A number of them carried long guns and pistols. Around three dozen members of a "self-styled militia," dressed in camouflage and carrying semiautomatic weapons, claimed to be there "to keep the peace." Anti-fascist counterprotesters, some of whom carried sticks and

The Unite the Right rally in Charlottesville, Virginia, on August 12, 2017, was billed as a call to arms to defend the removal of the monument to Robert E. Lee in that city. In truth, the event was intended to build support for a white nationalist movement. One consequence of the rally was greater scrutiny of Confederate monuments and increased calls for removals throughout the South.
(Jackie Zimmerman/Mercandotti Photo)

shields, traded insults with rally-goers, one of whom was heard yelling, "Dylann Roof was a hero!" There were unarmed peaceful protesters, too, including civil right leaders, members of church groups, and local residents. Even as the event grew hostile and fights broke out, police noticeably did not immediately step in to disperse the crowd. Governor McAuliffe, however, declared a state of emergency, saying he was "disgusted by the hatred and bigotry." His action prevented the noon rally from going forward.[24]

162   Nevertheless, tensions continued, as white supremacists and

counterprotesters clashed on side streets throughout downtown. Then just after one o'clock, James Alex Fields Jr., a twenty-year-old from Ohio emboldened by the gathering of white nationalists, drove his Dodge Challenger directly into a crowd of people who had peacefully assembled to protest the rally, sending bodies flying into the air, critically injuring several people, and killing thirty-two-year-old Heather Heyer. In addition to Heyer's death, two state troopers were killed when their helicopter, meant to monitor activities in downtown Charlottesville, crashed.[25]

Once more, Confederate monuments entered the national conversation, but now in the context of a wave of explicit white nationalism. In President Donald Trump's initial statement issued on August 14 about what had transpired in Charlottesville, likely written by a member of his staff, he said, "We condemn in the strongest possible terms this egregious display of hatred, bigotry, and violence on many sides. On many sides." Former Klan leader David Duke, who was in Charlottesville on Saturday, snapped back. "I would recommend you take a good look in the mirror and remember it was White Americans who put you in the presidency, not radical leftists," he wrote. Certainly, there were people at the rally who shared the beliefs of one Pennsylvania resident and self-proclaimed Nazi, who said that Trump's election had "emboldened" him and others who shared his white supremacist views. Nonetheless, it appeared that this display of violent white nationalism had crossed a red line for the new administration.[26]

President Trump backtracked on his initial statement one day later. Standing in the lobby of Trump Tower in New York, he appeared to defend the white nationalists by including them in the statement, "You had some very fine people on both sides." He continued, "Many of those people were there to protest the taking down of the statue of Robert E. Lee. . . . This week, it is Robert E. Lee. And I notice that Stonewall Jackson is coming down. I wonder, is it George Washington next? And is it Thomas Jefferson the week after? You know, you have to ask yourself, where does it stop?"[27]

Trump's remarks were roundly condemned, not only for including racist white nationalists in his description of "very fine people" but also for suggesting that Confederate monuments were equivalent to those paying tribute to the founding fathers. In truth, Confederate monuments had for over a century been linked to white supremacy, which is why white nationalists who rallied in Charlottesville were not there because of a nostalgia for the Confederacy. Many had no Confederate ancestry, nor were they Southern. They arrived angry about being displaced, or perhaps replaced, by immigrants, by women, by African Americans, by anyone who, in effect, challenged white male patriarchy. They saw the potential removal of the Lee monument as a siren call for their movement. What they did not anticipate is that the public outcry over what happened in Charlottesville would actually contribute to increased scrutiny and public education on the history of monuments, which hastened the movement to remove them.[28]

■ ■ ■

The aftermath of the Unite the Right rally, also known as the Charlottesville uprising, saw the renewal of a national debate over the meaning of Confederate monuments and what should be done about them. Almost immediately, Baltimore mayor Catherine Pugh had the city's Confederate monuments removed in the dead of night, citing issues of safety and security.[29] A few months later, the City of Memphis found a way around Tennessee's monument law, which prohibited removing the Nathan Bedford Forrest statue from public property. Instead, city leaders legally conveyed the land to a private entity called Memphis Greenspace, Inc. Because the state law applied only to publicly owned land, the new landowner was legally free to remove the statue, which it promptly did in December 2017. Caught off guard, the state legislature voted to remove $250,000 earmarked for the city's bicentennial and in 2018 amended the state's heritage protection law to impose financial penalties on any city that tried to remove a statue and to prohibit the strategy used by Memphis. It also allowed private citizens to sue their local government if it violated the law.[30]

Nonetheless, cities moved forward in trying to address Confederate monuments in the face of prohibitive legislation. The deadly violence that occurred in Charleston and again in Charlottesville required it. On June 22, 2017, Richmond mayor Levar Stoney announced the formation of the Monument Avenue Commission to correct the "false narrative" conveyed by the statues found along the historic thoroughfare. As he put it, the monuments not only "lionize the architects and defenders of slavery, but [perpetuate] the tyranny and terror of Jim Crow and reassert a new era of white supremacy." The commission was charged with finding new ways to address the inequality represented on the landscape, even if it meant "new signage and perhaps additional monuments."[31] In August 2017, Louisville mayor Greg Fischer announced that he had charged the city's Commission on Public Art to identify monuments and other works of public art "that could be interpreted as honoring bigotry, racism, and/or slavery." This was a first step. What to do with the monuments identified as racist involved another process.[32] And in October, Atlanta mayor Kasim Reed appointed members to the Advisory Committee on Confederate Monuments and City Street Names to review and make recommendations.[33]

Still, grassroots activists regarded these moves as far too moderate. Phil Wilayto, an organizer for Virginia Defenders for Freedom, Justice and Equality, felt Mayor Stoney was "dodging the issue completely."[34] And when Georgia governor Brian Kemp signed his state's monument bill into law preventing the removal of Confederate monuments in 2019, Atlanta's Advisory Committee felt it was left no option but to add contextual panels to the city's Confederate monuments. Sheffield Hale, a member of the Mayor's Committee as well as president and chief executive of the Atlanta History Center, which paid for the contextual panels, thought such exhibits stationed alongside Confederate statues moved conversations about race forward. But Richard Rose, president of Atlanta's NAACP, pushed back, arguing that additional markers do nothing more than "establish racism as valid." Like monument critics around the South who believed that the time for context markers was over, Rose stated, "You can't contextualize racism or compromise on racism."[35]

Richmond's Monument Avenue Commission and the Public Art and Monuments Advisory Committee in Louisville issued their reports in 2018, but they amounted to nothing more than a set of nonbinding recommendations. State monument laws remained an obstacle to removal. Not only were local communities overruled, but many of the states in which they were passed were controlled by Republican-dominated legislatures whose members came into office as a result of gerrymandering. This means of voter suppression meant that even Confederate monuments became untouchable, since a broad coalition of voters who wanted to change the laws were effectively being disfranchised.

Voter suppression, in fact, is key to understanding not only the current state of Confederate monuments but also the battle over their construction in the late nineteenth century. When the monument to Robert E. Lee was unveiled in Richmond in 1890, African Americans in that city recognized it as a symbol of their own oppression and its link to suppressing their right to vote. Barely a week after the unveiling of the Lee monument, John Mitchell Jr., the editor of the black newspaper the *Richmond Planet*, penned an editorial in which he warned readers that the rights that blacks had won during Reconstruction were being rolled back, especially the right to vote. "No species of political crimes has been worse than that which wiped the names of thousands of *bona-fide* Colored Republican voters from the Registration books of this state," Mitchell wrote. He claimed, rightly, that refusing to allow black men to vote was a "direct violation of the law" and blamed state officials sworn to uphold the U.S. Constitution for illegally scrubbing the names of men from voter rolls, marking them "dead" or as having moved to another state, when neither was true. Mitchell's words were prophetic as he identified what was essentially a backlash against racial progress.[36]

This has also been the story of Confederate monuments. For every forward step made to address this issue head-on, political machinations have reversed that progress. The changes to the Voting Rights Act in 2013 represented yet another step backward in the ongoing fight for racial justice and one that is critical to our historical and contemporary understanding of Confederate monuments. By suppressing the rights of black voters, as well as of white voters who support this movement, conservative-led state legislatures not only have prevented these voters from exercising their rights as citizens but have usurped local control to remove monuments legally. In doing so, they have left voters no other option for redressing this issue than to demonstrate their frustration by vandalizing and pulling down statues illegally.

Only two days after the events in Charlottesville, on August 14, 2017, this is exactly what happened. Protesters in Durham, North Carolina, went to the Confederate monument that sat adjacent to the Durham County Courthouse and swiftly yanked it to the ground. One year later, on August 20, 2018, protesters on the campus of the University of North Carolina ripped the controversial Confederate statue known as "Silent Sam" off of its pedestal. These two prominent examples of grassroots direct action signaled a new development in the history of these controversial statues. The long history of the push and pull of defending Confederate monuments and removing them was now at a crossroads.

Then in the summer of 2020, it erupted all over again.

EPILOGUE

The murder of George Floyd by Minneapolis police on May 25, 2020, and the video evidence that circulated in the aftermath, set off an enormous wave of Black Lives Matter demonstrations involving hundreds of thousands of people worldwide. In the American South, as well as in Europe, protesters not only registered their fury over police brutality and systemic racism but also fixed their attention on long-standing monuments to slave traders, slave owners, and white supremacy. While police killings of black men and women have regularly sparked outrage and protest in recent years, grief and rage over Floyd's death powered an unprecedented, sweeping response. These events also intensified the rhetoric around Confederate monuments, but the dynamics that had been in place since 2015 were still at play: as some government officials tried to outmaneuver popular will, local groups filed lawsuits to prevent removal based on state monument laws. Regardless, these public protests forced the issue, and in the days and weeks following Floyd's murder, several municipalities removed an unprecedented number of statues across the region.

Nowhere was the effect of these protests more intense than in Richmond, Virginia, home to Monument Avenue. Beginning on the evening of May 31, 2020, protesters targeted the monuments to Stonewall Jackson and Jefferson Davis and especially the large equestrian statue of Robert E. Lee.[1] The statue of Davis, part of a memorial that also included a sixty-five-foot Doric column along with a semicircle of thirteen columns representing each Confederate state, was ripped off of its pedestal. Along with the equestrian statue of Stonewall Jackson, the remains of the Davis memorial were spray-painted with slogans of protest. Yet it was Lee's statue that stood out.

As protests calmed, people continued to gather around the graffiti-sprayed monument for several days and nights. Tense standoffs with police were replaced by barbecue grills, music, children playing, and voter registration tables. Locals had reinterpreted the Lee monument through protest art and it swiftly became a tourist destination, a place to take photos and to see a new kind of history in action.[2] On June 8, 2020, locals projected an image of George Floyd onto the monument along with the slogans "No Justice, No Peace" and "BLM." Over the course of the summer, images of black leaders like Frederick Douglass, Harriet Tubman, W. E. B. Du Bois, and Georgia congressman John Lewis were projected onto the statue's pedestal, as were other victims of police violence, including Breonna Taylor. For many, it was the historical context that these Confederate icons long deserved.[3]

Statues were not the only target of Richmond's protesters; so, too, was the United Daughters of the Confederacy's headquarters. Its windows were knocked out and the building was set ablaze, damaging the interior. While not a monument in the form of a statue, the Daughters' headquarters officially functions as a memorial to the women of the Confederacy. But for local activists, the building represented the very organization responsible for the vast majority of statues dedicated to the Confederacy throughout the South and beyond. That it was attacked by the same protestors who targeted the Lee monument suggests that they understood the UDC's home base to be just as offensive as the statues the Daughters erected.[4]

The history of the United Daughters of the Confederacy and what, precisely, the organization stood for was now better known, at least among protesters, especially after events in Charlottesville only a few years before. Media outlets across the United States and around the world were intensely focused on the UDC's work of the early twentieth century, which in turn led to a better historical understanding of its role in propping up white supremacy. Such public scrutiny was more than the modern UDC could take. Aside from issuing a brief statement on the organization's website in August 2017 and another general statement on December

1, 2018, both of which condemned the actions of those they saw as using Confederate heritage for a hateful cause, the Daughters have remained silent and have refused to give media interviews, even after the vandalism of their headquarters. While some local chapters of the UDC have fought back by filing lawsuits or requesting restraining orders against monument removal in the face of local decisions, on the whole the organization's silence speaks volumes about how it is now a shell of its former self.[5]

What began in Richmond in late May spread across the South, as people took to the streets to protest monuments, spray paint them with graffiti, and demand their removal. Surprisingly, even in the face of state monument laws, communities began the process of removal. In North Carolina, the state's law provided a loophole to take down statues in the event their existence became an issue of public safety, and some local governments used it to justify removal. Likewise, on June 20, 2020, Governor Roy Cooper employed that loophole when he called for the removal of Confederate monuments from the grounds of the State Capitol.[6] Some towns, like Salisbury, worked out a deal with the local chapter of the UDC to move its monument to a cemetery. Virginia towns and cities led the region in the number of removals, in part because the state's law had been reversed to give back control to local governments beginning July 1, 2020. Richmond mayor Levar Stoney did not hesitate to act on the new law, taking down the monument to Stonewall Jackson on the very same day the law changed. Other local governments across the state followed suit.[7]

But the summer of 2020 did not spell the end of Confederate monuments in the South. Though several statues were removed, hundreds remained firmly in place, protected by police, local governments and state legislatures, self-appointed militias, and heritage laws. In some cases, lawsuits were filed to prevent local governments from removing monuments, keeping the issue in limbo and stoking even more divisiveness within communities. In an unusual case, the weather intervened in Lake Charles, Louisiana, in late August 2020 when Hurricane Laura toppled a Confederate statue that sat atop of its pedestal. The statue had survived years of protests but not Mother Nature.[8]

Given that 2020 was an election year, it is perhaps unsurprising that the GOP attempted to use this wave of monument activism to fuel a culture war on a national level. On July 3, President Trump issued an executive order to create a "National Garden of American Heroes." The order grouped together the protesters who had vandalized or destroyed monuments with the local governments that had also worked to remove them and suggested that "to destroy a monument is to desecrate our common inheritance." In truth, many monuments had been removed without incident, but the president sought to use such actions to sow seeds of division. More importantly, Confederate monuments are not a "common inheritance," and rather than bring people together, they are divisive. The order committed the federal government to build even more monuments. Ironically, statues of all but one of the individuals named in the executive order for this proposed garden of heroes — founding fathers, Davy Crockett, Harriet Tubman, and Booker T. Washington, among several others — already exist in cities and states across the country.[9]

One of the lines in Trump's executive order, if read differently, actually supports the removal of Confederate monuments. "These statues are silent teachers in solid form of stone and metal," the order reads, which is very similar to what critics of Confederate monuments have said since they were first built. The statement lends credence to the idea that monuments are tools employed to teach citizens about any number of values and belief systems, and in the case of the South, those have long included racism and white supremacy. So, if Americans on both sides of the monument debate agree that "statues are silent teachers," what, then, is the source of our divide?

The disconnect stems from how our shared history has been distorted in favor of a mythological narrative that separates us as Americans, and separates southerners even more so. The South, in particular, has been a hostage to Lost Cause rhetoric since the end of the Civil War. It was a powerful narrative to which white northerners capitulated in the nineteenth century and one that influenced the young minds of generations of white southerners, either because of what they learned in school or intuitively through southern culture, which has long honored the symbols of the Confederacy.

In the thick of the debates over monument removal in the summer of 2020, I sat down with Harvey Gantt, the well-respected black political figure who had long ago been part of the movement to challenge monuments. Our conversation began with a discussion of the debate over placing a Confederate monument in Charlotte on the grounds of city hall in 1977 and his opposition to it. Eventually, we settled into talking about the very important role that history education has in how we see the past—and sometimes past one another.

In the segregated public schools of the Jim Crow South, African American students learned a history of the Civil War and slavery that pushed back against the Lost Cause narrative. As Gantt told me, his high school teachers offered him what they said was an "alternative history" of the Civil War and slavery. The alternative, in this case, was a corrective to the myths of the Confederate tradition. As a child, he recalled, he did not pay any attention to the southern monuments that existed in his hometown of Charleston, but as he grew older that changed. "As you started to understand your ancestors were slaves . . . and what that has meant to you, has meant to your family, how my father couldn't go to high school, because of slavery, followed by Reconstruction, followed by Jim Crowism, separate but equal, all [meant to send] messages of who we are," he said, "then you begin to question the people who perpetrated this." Among his high school friends, they would ask one another, "Didn't America win the Civil War?"[10]

Growing up, Gantt learned and understood there were people who fought against his freedom and those who looked like him. "One of those people was someone from our community, John C. Calhoun," he said, hitting the table with his hand for emphasis as he recited each part of his name, adding "and with that tall monument in Marion Square" erected in his honor. The Civil War was everywhere in Charleston. "You could go to [Fort Sumter] and the Battery where the Civil War started," he said. "These were visceral. We could see these things as black kids growing up. And black kids understanding the 'alternative' history, the *true* history, started to say this [the Lost Cause narrative] is all wrong." He wondered aloud how his "white counterpart who is the same age" had learned "a certain history that makes [Confederate soldiers] seem noble" and "that [the war] was over states' rights." Thinking back, he recalled, "Even then I couldn't understand how they could see slavery as a good thing."[11]

What Harvey Gantt described to me in August 2020 helps explain why there is no common ground in the debate over Confederate monuments. In the simplest of terms, it's about competing versions of history. One is based in fact and the centrality of slavery to the Civil War and of white supremacy in the building of monuments. The other is based on a fabricated account of a battle over states' rights, stripped of the ugliness of slavery, which massages the truth as a means of dealing with Confederate defeat and regards monuments as honoring a just cause and virtuous heritage. For more than 150 years, this erroneous version of the past has dominated the culture of the South, but as the removal of monuments since 2015 suggests, the Lost Cause's days may be numbered. And with that, perhaps, there is common ground ahead.

ACKNOWLEDGMENTS

This is not a book I ever expected to write, although I had an inkling in the days after the Charlottesville uprising in 2017. The University of North Carolina Press, through my editor Brandon Proia, kept up the pressure to produce a book on the subject of Confederate monuments until I finally caved in late September 2019. To be fair, I had written several op-eds on the topic and had given more than two dozen talks over a two-year period. I also knew after my conversation with Brandon that I was going to say yes, but it didn't make writing this book an easy task. My research had to be expanded beyond the period I knew best, between 1865 and 1920, and cover the full breadth of the twentieth century and take into consideration the last twenty years. Historians generally don't work like this. They research a topic for a significant amount of time and only then do they write a book. Still, I had been thinking and writing about this subject on and off for several years and understood the contours of the debate. And here we are.

One of the reasons I accepted the challenge was the opportunity to be included in the Marcie Cohen Ferris and William R. Ferris Imprint at UNC Press, whose donors make books like mine possible. In addition to being wonderful scholars in the field of southern studies, Bill and Marcie are also some of the kindest and most generous people I've ever met in the academy. So, I am incredibly honored to be published through an imprint that bears their name.

No book comes to fruition without the help of others—friends, colleagues, fellow academics, students, archivists, and an entire team of people at UNC Press. Allow me to begin with the press. Brandon really put me through my paces with this one, but he is still my favorite editor and has my unwavering respect. John Sherer placed confidence in my ability to pull this off. Mark Simpson-Vos is always supportive, and I appreciate that more than he knows. Gina Mahalek, Dino Battista, Joanna Ruth Marsland, Susan Garrett, Dylan White, Jay Mazzocchi, Ann Bingham, Ellen

Bush, Anna Faison, Allie Shay, and Kim Bryant—I thank them for all that they do. I also want to thank Julie Bush, my copyeditor. She's outstanding.

It was important that I get the right information about Confederate monument data, since so many figures swirl in the news media. On that score, I want to thank Lecia Brooks and her team at the Southern Poverty Law Center in Montgomery, Alabama, for meeting with me and answering my questions, as well as Rachel Judge, a staff attorney with the Equal Justice Initiative, with whom I also met during my visit to Montgomery. Both organizations have made significant contributions to the general public's understanding of Confederate monuments and why they are worthy of our attention in the larger context of white supremacy and systemic racism. I also want to thank Carli Brosseau, a reporter with the *Raleigh News and Observer*, who offered some helpful data mining assistance in the early stages of this book.

At UNC Charlotte, where I've taught for nearly twenty years, I want to thank my history department colleagues for joining in a brown-bag discussion of a chapter and for the helpful feedback they provided. I especially want to give thanks to Ritika Prasad and Christine Haynes for their unflagging support and friendship. Christine and I joined the department the same year; she's a supremely talented scholar in modern French history. Ritika is one of the smartest people I know and an outstanding historian of South Asia. I'm lucky to have them as colleagues and friends. I'd also like to thank all of the students who took my senior research seminar on Confederate monuments, which I taught for the first time in Spring 2020. Despite the challenges presented by COVID-19 that led to an abrupt end to our in-class meetings, they wrote wonderful papers and inspired me to continue this work.

Some of my best friends come from the academy, many of whom I met through the Southern Association for Women Historians, if not the Southern Historical Association, and they have also been with me through this process. Alecia Long, Shannon Frystak, Danielle McGuire, and Heather Thompson—y'all are still my crew, even when we can't all be together in the same place at the same time. I also want to thank some awesome academic sisters who have shown support in social media spaces or in phone conversations, including Keri Leigh Merritt, Marjorie Spruill, Tammy Ingram, Malinda Lowery, and so many others. Françoise Hamlin, thank you for your friendship and for lending your expertise to a portion of this manuscript. Thanks, too, to Hilary Green, Adam Domby, and William Sturkey, with whom I've had important and thoughtful conversations around the issue of Confederate monuments. Their writing and public speaking on this subject are critical to our overall understanding of the meaning of these statues on the regional landscape. Thanks also to Angie Maxwell, who was instrumental in helping me understand GOP tactics in the South during the 1990s. A special shout-out goes to graduate students Julia Wall from the University of Alabama, whose research on a Confederate monument in her hometown of Douglasville, Georgia, I found inspiring, and Heather Haley of Auburn University. Heather provided valuable assistance with some photographic research at the Alabama Department of Archives and History that proved essential to this book.

Here in Charlotte I am grateful to friends with university ties whom I wish to thank for just being supportive friends, particularly Ashli Stokes and Amy Shehee. These two women, as they say in the South, are good people. Special thanks to Joanne Joy who shares my love for the South even when it breaks our heart. She read parts of the book and provided useful feedback. For that, I'm most appreciative. I also want to thank friends and neighbors here in the Queen City, including Mary McLaughlin, Kathryn Moczulski, Patt Snow, Annie Rivers, and the wonderful Kimi Pace.

As you can imagine, not everyone in my family was thrilled that I was writing about Confederate monuments. My mother, Flora Carter, worries about my safety, but she respects my work as a historian, and she loves me no matter what. Then there are those family members who are always cheerleaders, including my cousin Katura Crum and my sister Renita Hilse. While he's not a blood relative, Christopher Geissler is more than my friend, he's my Brother Man, and I'm forever grateful for his support and place in my life.

Last, I want to offer a special thank you to Harvey Gantt, a personal hero of mine. He generously gave an interview for this book, and my conversation with him will always stay with me. His respect for the study of history and its importance to civil conversation about controversial issues is one I wish more people shared.

I don't recommend writing in the middle of a pandemic. True, writing is a solitary process, but it's punctuated by time spent with friends and family. Not so much during the COVID-19 crisis. And online meetings are just not the same. Pets help, and I'm glad my pittie boy, Elbie, and my cat, Halen, were around to lighten the mood. One final point, and one that often appears in writers' acknowledgments and bears repeating—I take full responsibility for any errors that may appear in these pages. I've never worked so hard and on such a compressed timeline to complete a book, but I do believe that I did my best, and it's my hope that those who read it will learn from it and find it helpful to their understanding of Confederate monuments and their place in our shared history.

NOTES

INTRODUCTION

1. The state of North Carolina maintained the home until 1982.

2. "The Formal Opening of the Confederate Women's Home," *Fayetteville (N.C.) Observer*, November 24, 2015.

3. Cox, *Dixie's Daughters*.

4. In the 1896 *Plessy v. Ferguson* case, the U.S. Supreme Court upheld "separate but equal" segregation.

5. Of course, many towns and cities are bound by state monument laws whose legislatures saw fit to undermine local authority, making removal a far more challenging prospect.

6. President Trump's first executive order related to monuments were those on federal property. The "Executive Order on Protecting American Monuments, Memorials, and Statues and Combating Recent Criminal Violence," issued on June 26, 2020, went after states under Democratic leadership where, the order claims, "many State and local governments have lost the ability to distinguish between the lawful exercise of rights to free speech and assembly and unvarnished vandalism" and, further, had "surrendered to mob rule." See the White House website, https://www.whitehouse.gov/presidential-actions /executive-order-protecting-american-monuments-memorials-statues -combating-recent-criminal-violence/ (accessed July 26, 2020).

7. "N.C. Residents Support Keeping Confederate Monuments in Place," *Elon Poll—Confederate Statues and Monuments*, https://www.elon.edu/u/elon-poll /elon-poll-confederate-statues-and-monuments/ (accessed October 22, 2020).

8. "How George Floyd Was Killed in Police Custody," *New York Times*, May 31, 2020.

9. See "When White Women Wanted a Monument to Black 'Mammies,'" *New York Times*, February 6, 2020. This article originally stated there were 1,700 monuments but eventually corrected the figure to include all monuments, markers, and memorials. Articles that employ data mining of the SPLC data set include "Mapping the Hundreds of Confederate Statues across the U.S.," *Al Jazeera*, June 11, 2020, https://www.aljazeera.com/indepth/interactive/2020/06 /mapping-hundreds-confederate-statues-200610103154036.html; "Confederate Monuments Are Falling, but Hundreds Still Stand. Here's Where," *Washington Post*, July 2, 2020; and "Confederate Statues Were Never Really about Preserving History," *FiveThirtyEight*, July 8, 2020, https://projects.fivethirtyeight.com /confederate-statues/.

10. "Whose Heritage? Public Symbols of the Confederacy," Southern Poverty Law Center, https://www.splcenter.org/data-projects/whose-heritage (accessed March 1, 2020).

11. See, for example, Jeffrey Robinson's talk on Confederate monuments in which he (the ACLU's leading racial justice expert) claims there was an "explosion" of monument building during the height of the civil rights movement. "The Removal of Confederate Monuments: The Truth about the Confederacy," Youtube.com, https://www.youtube.com/watch?v=UkvVRIUV8-0 (accessed July 12, 2020).

12. "Confederate Iconography in the 20th Century," Equal Justice Initiative, https://segregationinamerica.eji.org/report/confederate-icongraphy.html (accessed March 1, 2020). In this report, the Equal Justice Initiative claims that there were "scores of new monuments" built at midcentury, but there is no link or evidence for this assertion.

13. "Confederate Monuments Are Falling, but Hundreds Still Stand. Here's Where."

14. With thanks to Dr. Kevin Cosby, an inspirational leader, pastor, and the president of Simmons College in Louisville.

15. "Taking a Knee and Taking Down a Monument," *New York Times*, February 3, 2018. Private messages between Ms. Bell and me were conducted via Facebook Messenger in 2018 and 2019.

16. See, for example, Thomas J. Brown, *Civil War Monuments and the Militarization of America* and *Public Art of Civil War Commemoration*; Clinton et al., *Confederate Statues and Memorialization*; and Domby, *False Cause*.

CHAPTER 1

1. On this point, see Merritt, *Masterless Men*, 286–322. As she notes, poor whites were in conflict with the desires of the southern slaveocracy.

2. Malinda Maynor Lowery, "We Are the Original Southerners," *New York Times*, May 22, 2018.

3. Rose, *Ku Klux Klan or Invisible Empire*, 51, 69.

4. Pollard, *Lost Cause*, 728–29; Maddex, *Reconstruction of Edward A. Pollard*, 19, 37.

5. Pollard, *Black Diamonds*, 38.

6. Ibid., 81, 83 (emphasis in original).

7. Maddex, *Reconstruction of Edward A. Pollard*, 40–42.

8. Pollard, *Lost Cause*, 729.

9. Ibid.,729.

10. Text source is Col. Samuel Thomas, Assistant Commissioner, Bureau of Refugees, *Freedmen and Abandoned Lands*, in 39th Cong., 1 Sess., Senate Exec. Doc. 2 (1865), online version available at http://www.digitalhistory.uh.edu/disp_textbook.cfm?smtID=3&psid=4560 (accessed November 2, 2019).

11. Ifill, *On the Courthouse Lawn*, 8–9, 16–17.

12. Alexander Stephens, "Cornerstone Speech," March 21, 1861, American Battlefield Trust, https://www.battlefields.org/learn/primary-sources/cornerstone-speech (accessed November 26, 2019).

13. Quote contained in "Rebecca Latimer Felton, 1835–1930" *New Georgia Encyclopedia*, https://www.georgiaencyclopedia.org/articles/history

-archaeology/rebecca-latimer-felton-1835-1930 (accessed November 28, 2019).

14. Data mined from the SPLC data set as documented in Ryan Best, "Confederate Statues Were Never Really about Preserving History," *FiveThirtyEight*, https://projects.fivethirtyeight.com/confederate-statues/.

15. "Richard Spencer: 'Charlottesville Wouldn't Have Occurred without Trump,'" *The Hill*, May 14, 2019, https://thehill.com/blogs/blog-briefing-room /news/443666-richard-spencer-charlottesville-wouldnt-have-occurred-without.

CHAPTER 2

1. *Jewels of Virginia*, 6, 17, 20.
2. Ibid., 25.
3. Ibid., 39.
4. Ibid., 40.
5. Wilson, *Baptized in Blood*, x–xvii.
6. *Confederate Monument on Capitol Hill*, 6.
7. *Brief History of the Ladies' Memorial Association of Charleston*, 5.
8. Ibid., 6.
9. *A History of the Origin of Memorial Day*, 24.
10. *Memorials to the Memory of Mrs. Mary Amarinthia Snowden*, 5.
11. Ockenden quote from *Confederate Monument on Capitol Hill*, 5; *History of the Wake County Ladies Memorial Association*, 7–8.
12. *History of the Origin of Memorial Day*, 24.
13. Ibid., 25.
14. Ibid., 25. See also Whites, *The Civil War as a Crisis in Gender*, 160–63.
15. *Ceremonies in Augusta, Georgia*, 17.
16. On New Bern, see *Ladies' Memorial Association Confederate Memorial Addresses*, 6.
17. *Ceremonies in Augusta, Georgia*, 4–5.
18. Ibid., 3.
19. Ibid., 8.
20. Ibid., 8–9.
21. Ibid., 9–11.
22. Ibid., 9–10.
23. *Burlington Free Press*, May 3, 1875, and *Pittsburgh Daily Post*, April 28, 1875.
24. *Ceremonies in Augusta, Georgia*, 21.
25. Ibid.
26. Ibid., 22.
27. All calculations for monument values in 2020 are gathered from the "Historical Currency Converter" page, *Historical Statistics*, https://www .historicalstatistics.org/Currencyconverter.html (accessed January 20, 2020).
28. The initial quotation in 1866 is from the Lee Family Digital Archive, https://leefamilyarchive.org/papers/letters/transcripts-UVA/v076.html (accessed January 18, 2020). The second quotation, from 1869, is also from the

Lee Family Digital Archive, https://leefamilyarchive.org/9-family-papers/861
-robert-e-lee-to-david-mcconaughy-1869-august-5 (accessed January 18, 2020).

29. "History and Description of the Confederate Monument in Greenwood Cemetery of New Orleans from the 1930s," Louisiana Works Progress Administration, Louisiana Digital Library, https://louisianadigitallibrary.org /islandora/object/state-lwp%3A6396 (accessed January 20, 2020).

30. Ibid.

31. "History and Description of the Robert E. Lee Statue at Lee's Circle in New Orleans, Louisiana from the 1930s," Louisiana Works Progress Administration, Louisiana Public Library, https://louisianadigitallibrary.org /islandora/object/state-lwp%3A7938 (accessed January 20, 2020); see also "Alexander Doyle," *New Orleans Times-Democrat*, February 22, 1884.

32. "The Lee Monument," *New Orleans Times-Democrat*, February 7, 1884; "Unveiling the Statue," *New Orleans Daily Picayune*, February 21, 1884; *St. Joseph (La.) Tensas-Gazette*, February 23, 1884.

33. "Unveiling the Statue," *New Orleans Daily Picayune*, February 21, 1884.

34. Ibid.

35. *New Orleans Daily Picayune*, March 12, 1903.

36. *New Orleans Daily Picayune*, February 7, 1884.

37. On the battle between men and women over Richmond's Lee monument, see Janney, *Burying the Dead but Not the Past*, 114–18. See also "On Monument Avenue," American Civil War Museum, October 9, 2017, https://acwm.org /blog/monument-avenue-what-mean-ye-monument.

38. *Richmond Dispatch*, May 25, 1890.

39. "Conquered Though Not Vanquished," *Richmond Times*, May 28, 1890.

40. Cox, *Dixie's Daughters*, 28–48.

41. Ibid., 38.

42. Information on the Daughters' agenda is drawn from Cox, *Dixie's Daughters*.

43. *Confederate Monument on Capitol Hill*, 11–21.

44. Ibid., 25–28, 35, 41–42.

45. Ibid., 55, 60, 65.

46. See chapters 6 and 7 of Cox, *Dixie's Daughters*.

47. Details on the numbers of monuments built can be found in the SPLC data set on monuments: https://docs.google.com/spreadsheets/d /17ps4aqRyaIfpu7KdGsy2HRZaaQiXUfLrpUbaR9yS51E/edit#gid=222998983 (accessed January 29, 2020). On the costs of monuments, see Cox, *Dixie's Daughters*, 56–57.

48. McNeel Marble Company advertisement, *Confederate Veteran*, February 1913.

49. Cox, *Dixie's Daughters*, 78, 89–90; Thomas J. Brown, *Civil War Monuments and the Militarization of America*, 105–16.

50. Edgar Leslie and Harry Ruby, "The Dixie Volunteers," 1917, IN Harmony: Sheet Music, Indiana University, http://webapp1.dlib.indiana.edu/metsnav /inharmony/navigate.do?oid=http://fedora.dlib.indiana.edu/fedora/get /iudl:290803/METADATA (accessed January 20, 2020).

51. *Address of Justice Heriot Clarkson*, 1–2.

52. Ibid., 3–4.

53. Ibid., 4–5.

CHAPTER 3

1. *Jackson (Miss.) Clarion-Ledger*, September 21, 1955. On the Till trial, see Tyson, *The Blood of Emmett Till*.

2. Rosa Parks's reaction to Till's murder is discussed in Tell, *Remembering Emmett Till*, 1.

3. *Tallahatchie (Miss.) Herald*, July 4, 1913.

4. Frederick Douglass, "Bombast," *New National Era* (Washington, D.C.), November 10, 1870.

5. Blight, "For Something beyond the Battlefield," 1169.

6. Kytle and Roberts, *Denmark Vesey's Garden*, 101–10; Fields, *Lemon Swamp*, 57.

7. According to historian Hilary Green, while children, teens, and young adults might make fun of a monument or deface one, older adults were less likely to take such risks. Email with author, September 12, 2020.

8. "The Lee Monument Unveiled," *Richmond Planet*, May 31, 1890.

9. "What of Virginia," *Richmond Planet*, June 7, 1890.

10. "The Voices of the Colored Press," *Richmond Planet*, June 14, 1890.

11. "Girl Sold for $416 in Year of 1846," *Chicago Defender*, March 6, 1920.

12. "Tear the Spirit of the Confederacy from the South," *Chicago Defender*, July 16, 1921.

13. Ibid.

14. Roscoe Simmons, "This Week," *Chicago Defender*, November 4, 1922.

15. Roscoe Simmons, "This Week," *Chicago Defender*, April 28, 1923.

16. "What Do You Say about It?," *Chicago Defender*, September 10, 1932.

17. Ibid.

18. See, for example, "Vandals at Monroe Mutilate Confederate Monument," *Shreveport Times*, November 10, 1896.

19. Du Bois, "Perfect Vacation," 279.

20. Lucius Harper, "Dustin' Off the News," *Chicago Defender*, December 7, 1940. For more on Camp Forrest, see the website for Arnold Air Force Base, https://www.arnold.af.mil/About-Us/Fact-Sheets/Display/Article/409311/camp-forrest/ (accessed April 23, 2020).

21. Dewey W. Grantham, "The South and Congressional Politics," in McMillen, *Remaking Dixie*, 25, 30, 31.

22. McMillen, *Remaking Dixie*, xv.

23. James R. Cobb, "World War II and the Mind of the Modern South," in McMillen, *Remaking Dixie*, 6–7.

24. "The Inaugural Address of Governor George C. Wallace, January 14, 1963," Alabama Department of Archives and History Digital Collection, https://digital.archives.alabama.gov/digital/collection/voices/id/2952 (accessed October 22, 2020).

25. "Civil War 'Played' at Modern High Costs," *Chicago Defender*, April 10, 1961.

26. While press accounts have perpetuated the narrative that monument building during the civil rights era represented a "spike," the truth is that most monuments were built during the 1890–1920 period. The figure of thirty-four monuments is drawn from the data set provided by the Southern Poverty Law Center; see https://www.splcenter.org/20190201/whose-heritage-public -symbols-confederacy (accessed April 1, 2020).

27. On stereotypes in television, see Cox, *Dreaming of Dixie*, 165–66.

28. "UDC Selects Headquarters in Richmond," *Richmond Times-Dispatch*, November 11, 1949.

29. "UDC Defers Decision on Headquarters," *Newport News (Va.) Daily Press*, November 17, 1950.

30. "Confederate Ball Finances Expected to Split Even," *Richmond Times-Dispatch*, January 23, 1954.

31. "Plans Approved for UDC Memorial," *Richmond Times-Dispatch*, February 11, 1954.

32. On the Gray commission, see Pratt, *The Color of Their Skin*.

33. "Memorial to Confederate Women Is Rapidly Becoming Realized," *Richmond Times-Dispatch*, December 14, 1956; "Memorial Building," United Daughters of the Confederacy, https://hqudc.org/memorial-building-2/ (accessed February 21, 2020).

34. "UDC Lauds Va., N.C., Ala. for Work in Education," *Newport News Daily Press*, November 13, 1957.

35. "'God First in Every Life' Is Theme for the Year," *Miami Herald*, November 10, 1954. See also "Challenge against Communism Opens UDC General Session," *Richmond Times-Dispatch*, November 10, 1954.

36. On citizens' councils, see McMillen, *Citizens' Council*; and Rolph, *Resisting Equality*.

37. "Editor Tells UDC States' Rights Threat, Threat to Freedom," *Greeneville (Tenn.) Sun*, October 10, 1956; "Attorney Discusses 'States Rights' at UDC Meeting," *Greenville (S.C.) News*, October 27, 1955.

38. Useful sources on the Civil War centennial include Cook, *Troubled Commemoration*; and Blight, *American Oracle*.

39. Cook, *Troubled Commemoration*, 69–71. On the Virginia centennial, see "Unity of Nation Stressed in Opening of Civil War Centennial at Richmond," *Kingsport (Tenn.) Times-News*, April 24, 1961; and Mary Mason Williams, *The Civil War Centennial and Public Memory in Virginia*, Virginia Center for Digital History, May 2005, http://www2.vcdh.virginia.edu/civilrightstv/essays/williams .pdf.

40. On state funding, see Cook, *Troubled Commemoration*, 65, 69; and Warrick, "'Mississippi's Greatest Hour,'" 96–97.

41. *Civil War Centennial: A Report to Congress*, 6.

42. "Dr. Reddick Blasts Glorifying the Civil War," *Chicago Defender*, May 2, 1961. See also "Lawrence Dunbar Reddick," *King Encyclopedia*, Stanford University, https://kinginstitute.stanford.edu/encyclopedia/reddick

-lawrence-dunbar (accessed April 15, 2020); and Reddick, *Crusader without Violence*.

43. "Unity of Nation Stressed in Opening of Civil War Centennial at Richmond."

44. "Alabama's Confederate Monument for Vicksburg," *Selma Times-Journal*, April 23, 1950; "Rebel Rally Features N.C. Field Rites," *Gettysburg Times*, July 2, 1963.

45. "Confederate Heroes Honored at Rites Here Today," *Selma Times-Journal*, April 26, 1955.

46. "Patterson Speaks in Vicksburg," *Jackson Clarion-Ledger*, April 29, 1957.

47. "Fairview Celebration Honors Jefferson Davis," *Louisville Courier-Journal*, June 4, 1957.

48. "Little Rock Refugees Help Shake Off Northern Bonds," *Jackson Clarion-Ledger*, April 13, 1958.

49. "Little Rock Refugees Help Shake Off Northern Bonds"; on the King case, see Eagles, *Price of Defiance*, 89–98.

50. "Noisy Crowd Is Ejected in Rare Move," *Lubbock Morning Avalanche*, May 3, 1957.

51. Ibid.

52. Ibid.; on segregation in Texas, see "Segregation," *Handbook of Texas*, Texas State Historical Association, https://tshaonline.org/handbook/online/articles/pks01 (accessed March 1, 2020).

53. Historical accounts of the Ole Miss Riot of 1962 include Eagles, *Price of Defiance*; Mickey, *Paths Out of Dixie*; and Meredith's own account, *Three Years in Mississippi*. Quotes from Kennedy and Barnett are from Al Kuettner, "Oxford, Mississippi—Anatomy of a Riot," *Chicago Defender*, October 13, 1962, 17.

54. Kuettner, "Oxford, Mississippi—Anatomy of a Riot."

55. John Neff, Jarod Roll, and Anne Twitty, "A Brief Historical Contextualization of the Confederate Monument at the University of Mississippi," May 16, 2016, https://history.olemiss.edu/wp-content/uploads/sites/6/2017/08/A-Brief-Historical-Contextualization-of-the-Confederate-Monument-at-the-University-of-Mississippi.pdf.

56. Mickey, *Paths Out of Dixie*, 211.

57. Eagles, *Price of Defiance*, 345–46.

58. Sitton, "Negro at Mississippi U. as Barnett Yields," *New York Times*, October 1, 1962.

59. Kuettner, "Oxford, Mississippi—Anatomy of a Riot," 17.

60. Meredith, *Three Years in Mississippi*, 309.

61. Meredith, *Mission from God*, 234–36.

62. "Ole Miss Ex-Student Pleads Guilty to Tying Noose on Statue," *Mississippi Today*, March 24, 2016; "Before Ole Miss Student, James Meredith Wanted Own Statue Destroyed," *Christian Science Monitor*, March 28, 2015.

63. In July 2020, the University of Mississippi removed its Confederate monument from the entryway to campus with plans to place it in a Confederate cemetery in another part of campus. The monument had long been embroiled

in controversy, as were the site plans for the monument's new home, which many regard as a shrine to the statue as well as to the Lost Cause.

CHAPTER 4

1. Roy Wilkins, "Could Nixon Have Won?," *New York Amsterdam News*, April 7, 1962.

2. "Candidate Urges Ban on Rebel Flag," *New York Amsterdam News*, August 3, 1963. On how the flag was used to instill fear, see "Birmingham, Where the Rebel Flag Overshadows the Stars and Stripes," *New York Amsterdam News*, October 26, 1963. Regarding the Dickens bill, see "Riled Rebs Write re Flag Bill," *New York Amsterdam News*, March 7, 1964.

3. James Meredith often acted alone in the cause of civil rights. He did not seek out civil rights leaders when he integrated the University of Mississippi, nor did he consult them when he began his march from Memphis. He believed that he understood best how to confront white supremacy in Mississippi and resented the fanfare that surrounded movement leaders.

4. Goudsouzian, *Down to the Crossroads*, 16.

5. Ibid., 16–21.

6. Ibid., 22–26.

7. Ibid., 117.

8. "Meredith March Raises U.S. Flag in Miss. Square," *York (Pa.) Daily Record*, June 15, 1966.

9. On the use of prisoners in Belzoni, Mississippi, see "CR Hikers Camping in Pig Lot," *Jackson Clarion-Ledger*, June 21, 1966.

10. *Greenwood (Miss.) Commonwealth*, July 15, 1966.

11. Some estimates suggest there were 15,000 people when the Meredith March arrived in Jackson.

12. "12,000 End Rights March to Jackson," *New York Times*, June 27, 1966.

13. "10,000 Wind Up Thunderous Meredith March," *Chicago Defender*, June 27, 1966.

14. Details of Younge's life are drawn from Forman, *Sammy Younge, Jr.*

15. Ibid.

16. "Tuskegee Man Slain; 1500 Join Protest," *Chicago Defender*, January 5, 1966.

17. Forman, *Sammy Younge, Jr.*, 197–203.

18. Ibid., 206–7.

19. Ibid., 25.

20. Ibid., 29.

21. Ibid., 250.

22. Ibid., 252–53.

23. Ibid., 254.

24. White-owned newspapers reported on events in Tuskegee after the verdict by calling the situation a "riot" and the students a "mob." See "Verdict Puts Mob in Frenzy," *Central New Jersey Home News*, December 9, 1966; and "Alabama Negro Students Riot to Protest Man's Acquittal," *Tampa Tribune*, December 10, 1966.

25. "Chapters Announce Secession from U.S. for KA 'Old South Ball' Held in Raleigh," *Daily Tar Heel* (Chapel Hill, N.C.), February 6, 1949. On Charlotte, see "Old South Ball, Sweetheart and Alumni," *Daily Tar Heel*, April 11, 1958; "Roses of Kappa Alpha to Be Chosen Tonight as Old South Lives Again," *Charlotte (N.C.) Observer*, April 12, 1958; and "Ol' South Done Rose Once Mo'!," *Charlotte Observer*, April 13, 1958. At UNC, see "South Rises Again . . . Briefly," *Daily Tar Heel*, March 30, 1969.

26. "South Rises Again . . . Briefly."

27. Nicholas Graham, "Historic African American Enrollment at UNC," *History on the Hill* (blog), April 21, 2016, https://blogs.lib.unc.edu/hill/index .php/2016/04/21/historic-african-american-enrollment-at-unc/.

28. "Wallace Will 'Sit around Confederate Monument,'" *Wilkes-Barre Leader*, November 7, 1968.

29. "Agnew Mellow in Talk Hailing Confederate Heroes," *New York Times*, May 10, 1970.

30. Bruce E. Stewart, "Stone Mountain," *New Georgia Encyclopedia*, May 25, 2005, last updated October 31, 2016, https://www.georgiaencyclopedia.org /articles/geography-environment/stone-mountain.

31. Ibid.

32. "Brave Woman Fights City Fathers to Decorate Monument," *Fort Lauderdale News*, May 31, 1974; "Confederate Battle of Marian Rawls," *Kingsport Times*, May 31, 1974. The issue of land ownership has been at the center of more recent battles over possible monument removal.

33. "Harvey Gantt," City of Charlotte — Past Mayors, https://charlottenc .gov/Mayor/PastMayors/Pages/HarveyGantt.aspx (accessed May 8, 2020); "Harvey B. Gantt," South Carolina African American History Calendar, https://scafricanamerican.com/honorees/harvey-b-gantt/ (accessed May 8, 2020).

34. Charlotte (N.C.) City Council Minutes, May 16, 1977, Minute Book 65, 256; quotes from Walker in "Council to Rule on Marker," *Charlotte Observer*, May 18, 1977.

35. Charlotte City Council Minutes, May 16, 1977, 256.

36. Ibid.

37. Ibid.

38. Ibid., 257.

39. Ibid.

40. Ibid.

41. Ibid. Walker's interview with the press appears in "Confederate Marker an Outrage to Gantt," *Charlotte Observer*, May 1, 1977.

42. Charlotte City Council Minutes, May 23, 1977, Minute Book 65, 291.

43. Ibid.

44. Ibid., 292–93.

45. Ibid., 293.

46. Ibid., 294.

47. Ibid.

48. Ibid.

49. Ibid.

50. Ibid.

51. Ibid.

52. Ibid.

53. Ibid., 296; "Confederate Memorial to Stay at City Hall," *Charlotte Observer*, May 24, 1977.

54. Harriet Doar, "We're Not Big on Statues: And It's a Little Late for This One," *Charlotte Observer*, May 25, 1977.

55. "Observer Forum," *Charlotte Observer*, May 28, 1977.

56. "Gantt Deserves Commendation," *Charlotte Observer*, June 4, 1977.

57. Larry Walker, "Can Gantt Be Fair to All Residents," *Charlotte Observer*, September 17, 1979.

CHAPTER 5

1. "Confederate Flag Flying is Urged During March," *Monroe News-Star*, June 23, 1966.

2. "NAACP Asks for Removal of Stars and Bars," *Los Angeles Times*, March 9, 1987. On the history of Confederate flags and their changing meaning, see Coski, *Confederate Battle Flag*.

3. David Treadwell, "Symbol of Racism? Confederate Flag: Battle Still Raging," *Los Angeles Times*, March 9, 1987.

4. Ibid. As a state representative, Holmes proposed a resolution to remove the Confederate battle flag from the dome of the Alabama State Capitol as early as 1975. See "New Battle Lines Appearing in the South over Confederate Flag's Racial Symbolism," *Albuquerque Journal*, March 14, 1987. The original article appeared in the *Christian Science Monitor*.

5. Allen Steed, "Dispute over Flag Disregards Full History," *Alabama Journal*, April 10, 1987; E. M. Moore, "Removal of Confederate Flag Could Open Floodgates," *Greenville (S.C.) News*, April 19, 1987; "Groover Stands by 1956 Flag Change," *Atlanta Voice*, April 11, 1987. See also William Brown's letter to the editor, "Real Reasons," *Newport News (Va.) Daily Press*, February 16, 1987, in which he worries about "the desire of some black groups to have the statues of Confederate soldiers removed from courthouse squares." South Carolina state senator Glenn McConnell also wrote a letter to the editor, "Keep the Confederate Flag Flying," *Orangeburg (S.C.) Times and Democrat*, June 12, 1986. McConnell served as president of the College of Charleston from 2014 to 2018.

6. The Caddo Parish Confederate monument was given protected status by the National Register of Historic Places. For more on its history, see the National Register of Historic Places Registration Form for the Caddo Parish Confederate Monument, National Park Service, https://www.nps.gov/nr/feature/places/pdfs/13001124.pdf (accessed June 1, 2020). See also "A Plan for Unity," editorial, *Shreveport Journal*, February 11, 1987.

7. "Rebel Flag Evokes Range of Emotions," *Shreveport Journal*, January 1, 1987.

8. "Confederate Flag: A Piece of History or Racist Taunt?," *Shreveport*

Journal, January 29, 1987; see also "25 Defend Confederate Flag before Caddo Commission," *Shreveport Journal*, January 29, 1987.

9. "A Plan for Unity," *Shreveport Journal*, February 11, 1987.

10. Ibid. The ongoing discussions about removal were reported in "History and Heritage Cannot Be Removed," *Shreveport Journal*, January 8, 1988; "Slavery an Element of Southern Growth," *Shreveport Journal*, January 22, 1988; and "Flag Honors Southern 'Lost Cause,'" *Shreveport Journal*, January 25, 1988.

11. "Black Leaders Should Address 'Real' Issues," *Shreveport Times*, January 15, 1989.

12. "Controversy Arises Again over Courthouse Confederate Flag," *Shreveport Journal*, February 23, 1989.

13. On political realignment, see Maxwell and Shields, *Long Southern Strategy*. I also appreciate my discussion with Angie Maxwell on how the politics of the 1990s likely shaped monument debates.

14. "White Separatists March in Alabama," *New York Times*, June 14, 1992; "Skinheads Demonstrate in Alabama," *Fort Worth Star-Telegram*, June 14, 1992. My discussion about the new southern heritage movement is informed by Prince, "Neo-Confederates in the Basement," 147–48. For more on the white power movement, see Belew, *Bring the War Home*.

15. Prince, "Neo-Confederates in the Basement," 148–53.

16. On the concept of the Lost Cause as a civil religion, see Wilson, *Baptized in Blood*.

17. Prince, "Neo-Confederates in the Basement," 157, 163–64, 165.

18. "Confederate Heritage Bashing Is Never the Answer," *The Tennessean*, January 3, 1993.

19. "The Symbol War," *Atlanta Constitution*, March 7, 1993

20. Ibid. In "Celebrating Old Divisions," *New Orleans Times-Picayune*, March 12, 1993, the paper calls the Liberty Place monument a "racial embarrassment." Notably, David Duke presided over the rededication.

21. In 2010, Burkhalter became Speaker of the Georgia House of Representatives, and in May 2020 he was tapped by President Donald J. Trump to become U.S. ambassador to Norway.

22. "Symbol War."

23. Ibid.

24. Ibid.

25. The interviews with historians formed a sidebar to the main article, "The Symbol War."

26. On the Greensboro bust of King, see "Martin Luther King, Jr. Monument, Greensboro," Commemorative Landscapes of North Carolina, https://docsouth.unc.edu/commland/monument/32/ (accessed June 6, 2020); and "Martin Luther King, Jr. Memorial Sculpture, Charlotte," Commemorative Landscapes of North Carolina, https://docsouth.unc.edu/commland /monument/355/ (accessed June 6, 2020).

27. "Richmond May Honor Ashe with Confederates: Statue Would Line Monument Avenue," *Baltimore Sun*, June 18, 1995.

28. "Monumental Stir: An Ashe Statue Roils the Waters in His Hometown," *Boston Globe*, June 30, 1995.

29. "On the Street Where Confederates Reign, Arthur Ashe May, Too," *New York Times*, June 18, 1995; "Race-Tinged Furor Stalls Arthur Ashe Memorial," *New York Times*, July 9, 1995. On the myth of black service to the Confederacy, see Levin, *Searching for Black Confederates*.

30. "Richmond Council Endorses Statue of Arthur Ashe," *New York Times*, July 19, 1995; "Tennis Great Ashe Honored," *Tampa Bay Times*, July 19, 1995.

31. "Arthur Ashe Statue Set Up in Richmond at Last," *New York Times*, July 5, 1996; "Ashe Statue Joins Those of Confederates," *New York Times*, July 11, 1996.

32. Carney, "'Most Manly in the World,'" 172–73; "Jack Kershaw, Stalwart of White Nationalism, Dies," *Hatewatch* (blog), Southern Poverty Law Center, https://www.splcenter.org/hatewatch/2010/09/24/jack-kershaw-stalwart-white-nationalism-dies (accessed June 10, 2020).

33. Carney, "'Most Manly in the World,'" 173, 180.

34. "Monument of Nathan Bedford Forrest Draws Protests," *Selma Times-Journal*, October 8, 2000.

35. "City Funded Controversial Monument," *Montgomery Advertiser*, October 14, 2020.

36. City of Selma, Alabama, Minutes of the City Council, Monday, November 13, 2000.

37. "Debate over Nathan Bedford Forrest Monument Continues to Raise Opinions," *Selma Times-Journal*, October 18, 2000.

38. "Parade Held to Preserve Monument," *Selma Times-Journal*, November 20, 2000. For more on H. K. Edgerton, see Levin, *Search for Black Confederates*, 152-153.

39. "Supporters of Forrest Monument Take to Streets," *Montgomery Advertiser*, November 20, 2000.

40. "Monument Is Headless," *Selma Times-Journal*, March 13, 2012; "Group Offers Reward in Theft of Bust," *Montgomery Advertiser*, March 28, 2012; "Improvement Plan to Give Confederate Circle 'New Look,'" *Montgomery Advertiser*, June 27, 2012; "Bust of Civil War General Stirs Anger in Alabama," *New York Times*, August 25, 2012.

41. "New Park May Balance Confederate Memorial," *Louisville Courier-Journal*, December 9, 2002. On the University of Louisville's involvement in the park's creation, see Dr. J. Blaine Hudson and Mitchell Payne to Dr. Tom Owen, October 14, 2003, in Freedom Park Reference File, University of Louisville Archives and Special Collections.

42. "New Park May Counterbalance Memorial." On Hudson, see "J. Blaine Hudson—an Inspiration," on the University of Louisville's website about Freedom Park, https://louisville.edu/freedompark/j.-blaine-hudson-an-inspiration (accessed June 13, 2020).

43. "Activists Renew Call to Remove Monument," *Louisville Courier-Journal*, February 22, 2005.

44. "Proposal to Remove Confederate Monument 'Preposterous,'" *Louisville Courier-Journal*, February 28, 2005.

45. "Plea to Remove Controversial Confederate Monument Debated," *Louisville Courier-Journal*, March 7, 2005.

46. Alicia Kelso, "City's Confederate Monument Removed from Campus," *UofL News*, November 22, 2016, http://www.uoflnews.com/post/uofltoday/citys -confederate-monument-removed-from-campus/.

47. "Norfolk Gets Its Confederate Soldier," *Staunton (Va.) News Leader*, January 6, 2007.

48. See SPLC data set, https://docs.google.com/spreadsheets/d /17ps4aqRyaIfpu7KdGsy2HRZaaQiXUfLrpUbaR9yS51E/edit#gid=222998983 (accessed June 19, 2020).

49. "Mississippi to Restore Jefferson Davis Monument," *Daily World* (Opelousas, La.), March 11, 2009. On the story of Jim Limber, see John Coski's essay, reprinted as "John Coski on Jefferson Davis and Jim Limber," *Civil War Memory* (blog), June 20, 2008, http://cwmemory.com/2008/06/20/john -coski-on-jefferson-davis-and-jim-limber/.

50. "Mississippi to Restore Jefferson Davis Monument," *Picayune (La.) Item*, March 11, 2009.

51. "Statue of Jefferson Davis Proposed," *Richmond Times-Dispatch*, June 10, 2008; Beauvoir: The Jefferson Davis Home and Library, https://www .visitbeauvoir.org/ (accessed June 20, 2020).

52. "Crist's Running Mate Defends Flag Role," *Tampa Bay Times*, September 19, 2006.

53. Ibid.

54. "Perry Defended Confederate Symbols," *Santa Fe New Mexican*, October 5, 2011.

55. Ibid.; Will Weissert, "Perry Once Defended Confederate Symbols," Boston.com, October 4, 2011, http://archive.boston.com/news/politics/articles /2011/10/04/perry_once_defended_confederate_symbols/.

CHAPTER 6

1. "'This Is Just Pure Evil at Work,'" *Baltimore Sun*, June 19, 2015; "9 Shooting Victims Remembered," *Charlotte Observer*, June 19, 2015; "Anguish over Church Killings," *New York Times*, June 19, 2015.

2. "Charleston Church Shooter Dylann Roof: 'I Wanted to Start a Race War,'" *Chicago Defender*, June 19, 2015.

3. "Spotlight on Supremacist Group," *New York Times*, June 24, 2015.

4. "Anguish Over Church Killings"; "From Ferguson to Charleston, Anguish about Race Keeps Building," *New York Times*, June 21, 2015.

5. "From Ferguson to Charleston, Anguish about Race Keeps Building"; "Charleston Shooting Revives Flag Debate," *New York Times*, June 22, 2015.

6. "From Ferguson to Charleston, Anguish about Race Keeps Building." On lynching near monuments, see Ifill, *On the Courthouse Lawn*.

7. "Officials Vow to Act against Symbols of Confederacy," *New York Times*, June 24, 2015. Lindsey Graham eventually urged the South Carolina legislature to remove the flag from capitol grounds. See "Symbol of Hatred," *New York*

Times, June 24, 2015. Cornell Brooks quoted in "Charleston Church Massacre Draws Crowds, Raises Questions," *Chicago Defender*, June 22, 2015.

8. "Two Charged in Flag Removal at Capitol," *New York Times*, June 28, 2015.

9. Ibid.

10. "South Carolina Settles Its Decades-Old Dispute over a Confederate Flag," *New York Times*, July 10, 2015.

11. "A General's Final Stand Divides a Southern City," *New York Times*, July 20, 2015.

12. Ibid.

13. Ibid. See also "Confederate Memorials and Racial Terror," *New York Times*, July 25, 2015.

14. *Tennessee Heritage Protection Act*, Tenn. Code Ann. § 4-1-412, https://www.tn.gov/content/dam/tn/environment/historic-commission /thc_heritageact_TENNESSEE%20CODE%20UNANNOTATED%20CUI _%20PAW%20Document%20Page.pdf (accessed June 26, 2020).

15. *South Carolina Heritage Protection Act*, HB 4895, South Carolina General Assembly, 113th Session, 1999–2000, https://www.scstatehouse.gov /sess113_1999–2000/bills/4895.htm (accessed June 26, 2020). On Virginia's law, see "Code of Virginia—Memorials for War Veterans," Virginia Law, https://law .lis.virginia.gov/vacode/title15.2/chapter18/section15.2–1812/ (accessed June 26, 2020). On McAuliffe's veto, see "After Charlottesville, Va. Democrats See Opening to Change 114-Year-Old Monuments Law," *Washington Post*, August 25, 2017.

16. "McCrory Signs Ban on Removing Historical Monuments," *Raleigh (N.C.) News and Observer*, July 23, 2015; "What's the Future for NC's Confederate Statues?," *Raleigh News and Observer*, August 14, 2017. North Carolina's original Senate bill on monuments passed in April 2015; see https://www.ncleg.gov/Sessions/2015/Bills/Senate/PDF/S22v3.pdf (accessed June 26, 2020). Wahlers, "North Carolina's Heritage Protection Act." For a good overview of the laws protecting Confederate monuments, see Phelps and Owley, "Etched in Stone."

17. "Monuments' Removal Challenged," *New York Times*, December 20, 2017.

18. Landrieu's speech was reprinted in several American newspapers but most notably in the *New York Times*. See "Mitch Landrieu's Speech on the Removal of Confederate Monuments in New Orleans," *New York Times*, May 23, 2017. The speech was also videotaped and can be viewed on YouTube, https://www.youtube.com/watch?v=csMbjGo-6Ak (accessed June 27, 2020).

19. "Mitch Landrieu's Speech on the Removal of Confederate Monuments in New Orleans," *New York Times*, May 23, 2017. Landrieu's speech, for example, showed an engagement with the findings of my book *Dixie's Daughters*.

20. *Alabama Memorial Preservation Act*, AL SB 60, 2017, LegiScan, https://legiscan.com/AL/text/SB60/id/1617687 (accessed June 27, 2020).

21. "Suit Filed against Charlottesville and City Council to Prevent Lee Statue Removal," *Richmond Times-Dispatch*, March 21, 2017. On vandalizing of monuments around the South, see, for example, in Richmond, "Confederate Statue Vandalized in Va.," WSPA News, June 25, 2015; and in Charlotte,

"Defaced Memorial Stirred Controversy from the Beginning," *Charlotte Observer*, June 24, 2015.

22. "White Nationalist Richard Spencer Leads Torch-Bearing Protesters Defending Lee Statue," *Washington Post*, May 14, 2017; "Richard Bertrand Spencer," Southern Poverty Law Center, https://www.splcenter.org/fighting -hate/extremist-files/individual/richard-bertrand-spencer-0 (accessed June 29, 2020).

23. "Recounting a Day of Rage, Hate, Violence and Death," *Washington Post*, August 14, 2017.

24. Ibid.

25. Ibid.; "One Dead as Car Strikes amid Protests of White Nationalists Gathering in Charlottesville; Two Die in Helicopter Crash," *Washington Post*, August 12, 2017.

26. "One Dead as Car Strikes amid Protests of White Nationalists Gathering in Charlottesville; Two Die in Helicopter Crash."

27. Rosie Gray, "Trump Defends White-Nationalist Protesters: 'Some Very Fine People on Both Sides,'" *The Atlantic*, August 15, 2017.

28. Karen L. Cox, "What Changed in Charlottesville," *New York Times*, August 11, 2019.

29. "Citing 'Safety and Security,' Pugh Has Baltimore Confederate Monuments Taken Down," *Baltimore Sun*, August 15, 2017; Kelly Swanson, "Baltimore Removed All 4 of Its Confederate Statues Overnight," *Vox*, August 16, 2017, https://www.vox.com/2017/8/16/16155844/baltimore-confederate -statues-remove-overnight (accessed June 25, 2020).

30. Phelps and Owley, "Etched in Stone," 660.

31. "Richmond Mayor Vows to Confront Tributes to Southern Civil War Figures," *Washington Post*, June 22, 2017.

32. "Process Announced for Identifying Public Art, Monuments That Could Be Seen as Honoring Bigotry, Racism, Slavery," LouisvilleKy.gov, https://louisvilleky.gov/news/process-announced-identifying-public-art -monuments-could-be-seen-honoring-bigotry-racism (accessed June 30, 2020).

33. David Pendered, "Mayor Reed Names Six to Advisory Committee on Confederate Streets, Statues," *Saporta Report*, October 2, 2017.

34. Wilayto quoted in "Richmond Mayor Vows to Confront Tributes to Southern Civil War Figures." See also Virginia Defenders for Freedom, Justice and Equality (blog), https://defendersfje.blogspot.com/ (accessed June 30, 2020).

35. "Atlanta's Confederate Monuments: How Do 'Context Markers' Help Explain Racism?," *The Guardian*, August 3, 2019.

36. Mitchell quote from "The Voices of the Colored Press," *Richmond Planet*, June 14, 1890.

EPILOGUE

1. "Robert E. Lee Statue and Daughters of Confederacy Building Attacked by Richmond Protesters," *Washington Post*, May 31, 2020.

2. "Robert E. Lee Monument Becomes Epicenter of Protest," Associated Press, July 2, 2020.

3. AP, "Image of George Floyd Projected over Confederate Statue," WUSA9, June 11, 2020, https://www.wusa9.com/article/news/nation-world/floyd-face-projected-confederate-monument/507-27098f96-5cac-44bb-bf67-8bf0ab05c568.

4. For more on what happened to the UDC headquarters, see Karen L. Cox, "Setting the Lost Cause on Fire," *Perspectives on History*, August 6, 2020, https://www.historians.org/publications-and-directories/perspectives-on-history/summer-2020/setting-the-lost-cause-on-fire-protesters-target-the-united-daughters-of-the-confederacy-headquarters.

5. Ibid. On UDC efforts to block removal, see "UDC Awarded Temporary Restraining Order against Statue Removal," *Chatham (N.C.) News Record*, November 1, 2019; and "Lawsuit Filed to Block Removal of Caddo Confederate Monument," *Shreveport Times*, October 20, 2017.

6. "NC Governor Orders Confederate Monuments Removed at Capitol after Statues Toppled," *Raleigh News and Observer*, June 20, 2020.

7. "Stonewall Jackson Removed from Richmond's Monument Avenue," *Washington Post*, July 1, 2020.

8. "This Confederate Monument Survived Protests, but Not the Hurricane," *New York Times*, August 27, 2020.

9. "Executive Order on Building and Rebuilding Monuments to American Heroes," July 3, 2020, https://www.whitehouse.gov/presidential-actions/executive-order-building-rebuilding-monuments-american-heroes/.

10. Harvey Gantt, interview with author, August 4, 2020.

11. Ibid.

BIBLIOGRAPHY

ARCHIVAL COLLECTIONS

Jackson, Miss.
  Mississippi Division of Archives and History
    Mars (Florence) Collection
Louisville, Ky.
  University of Louisville Archives and Special Collections
    Freedom Park Reference File
Montgomery, Alabama
  Alabama Department of Archives and History
    Jim Peppler Southern Courier Photograph Collection

NEWSPAPERS AND PERIODICALS

Alabama Journal
Albuquerque Journal
Al Jazeera
Atlanta Constitution
Atlanta Voice
The Atlantic
Baltimore Sun
Boston Globe
Burlington (Vt.) Free Press
Central New Jersey Home News
Charlotte (N.C.) Observer
Chatham (N.C.) News Record
Chicago Defender
Christian Science Monitor
Daily Tar Heel (Chapel Hill, N.C.)
Fayetteville (N.C.) Observer
Fort Lauderdale News
Fort Worth Star-Telegram
Gettysburg Times
Greeneville (Tenn.) Sun
Greenville (Miss.) News
Greenville (S.C.) News
Greenwood (Miss.) Commonwealth
The Guardian (U.K.)
The Hill
Jackson (Miss.) Clarion-Ledger

Kingsport (Tenn.) Times
Los Angeles Times
Louisville City News
Louisville Courier-Journal
Lubbock Morning Avalanche
Miami Herald
Mississippi Today
Monroe (La.) News-Star
Montgomery Advertiser
New National Era (Washington, D.C.)
New Orleans Daily Picayune
New Orleans Times-Democrat
New Orleans Times-Picayune
Newport News (Va.) Daily Press
New York Amsterdam News
New York Times
Opelousas (La.) Daily World
Orangeburg (S.C.) Times and Democrat
Picayune (La.) Item
Pittsburgh Courier
Pittsburgh Daily Post
Raleigh (N.C.) News and Observer
Richmond (Va.) Dispatch
Richmond (Va.) Planet
Richmond (Va.) Times-Dispatch
Santa Fe New Mexican
Saporta Report
Selma Times-Journal
Shreveport Journal
Shreveport Times
Staunton (Va.) News Leader
St. Joseph (La.)Tensas-Gazette
Tallahatchie (Miss.) Herald
Tampa Bay Times
Tampa Tribune
The Tennessean
University of Louisville News
Washington Post
York (Pa.) Daily Record

GOVERNMENT RECORDS

Charlotte (N.C.) City Council Minutes, 1936–1978
City of Selma, Alabama, Office of the City Clerk, Minutes of the City Council,
    2000

Address by Maj. John W. Moore Delivered at Oakwood Cemetery, May 10, 1881.
Raleigh, N.C.: Edwards, Broughton and Co., 1881.

Address of Hon. T. W. Mason before the Ladies' Memorial Association at the
Laying of the Cornerstone of the Confederate Monument. Raleigh, N.C.: E. M.
Uzzell, Printer and Binder, 1898.

Address of Justice Heriot Clarkson, at the Memorial Day Exercises of the Johnston-
Pettigrew Chapter, United Daughters of the Confederacy. Raleigh, N.C., 1933.

Address on the Life and Character of Maj. Gen. Stephen D. Ramseur before the
Ladies' Memorial Association of Raleigh, N.C. Raleigh, N.C.: E. M. Uzzell,
Steam Printer and Binder, 1891.

An Address Containing a Memoir of the Late Major-General William Henry Chase
Whiting. Raleigh, N.C.: Edwards and Broughton, Printers and Binders, 1895.

A Brief History of the Ladies' Memorial Association of Charleston, S.C.
Charleston: H. P. Cooke & Co., Printers, 1880.

Ceremonies in Augusta, Georgia, Laying the Corner Stone of the Confederate
Monument and the Unveiling and Dedication of the Monument. Augusta, Ga.:
Chronicle and Constitutionalist Job Printing Establishment, 1878.

Confederate Memorial Addresses, New Bern, N.C., May 11, 1885. Richmond, Va.:
Whittet and Shepperson, 1886.

The Confederate Monument on Capitol Hill, Montgomery, Alabama.
Montgomery: Ladies Memorial Association, 1898.

Confederate Veteran. Nashville, Tenn.: S. A. Cunningham, 1893–1913.

Hearing before Senate Executive Committee on Freedom and Abandoned Lands.
39th Cong., 1st sess., 1865.

A History of the Origin of Memorial Day as Adopted by the Ladies' Memorial
Association of Columbus, Georgia. Columbus: Thos. Gilbert, Printer and
Manufacturing Stationer, 1898.

History of the Wake County Ladies Memorial Association. Raleigh, N.C., 1938.

The Jewels of Virginia: A Lecture by Col. George Wythe Munford. Richmond, Va.:
Gary and Clemmitt, Printers, 1867.

Ladies' Memorial Association Confederate Memorial Addresses, May 11, 1885,
New Bern, N.C. Richmond, Va.: Whittet & Shepperson, 1886.

The Ladies Memorial Association of Montgomery, Alabama: The Origin and
Organization. Compiled by Marielou Armstrong Cory. Montgomery:
Alabama Printing Company, 1902.

Memorial Address upon the Life of General James Green Martin Delivered by
Hon. Walter Clark, Chief Justice of the Supreme Court of North Carolina.
Raleigh, N.C.: n.p., May 10, 1916.

Memorials to the Memory of Mrs. Mary Amarinthia Snowden Offered by Societies,
Associations, and Confederate Camps. Charleston, S.C.: Walker, Evans, and
Cogswell, Co., Printers, 1898.

Our Confederate Dead, souvenir publication of the Ladies Hollywood Memorial
Association. Richmond, Va.: Ladies Hollywood Memorial Association,
1916.

Pollard, Edward A. *Black Diamonds Gathered in the Darkey Homes of the South.* New York: Pudney and Russell, 1859.

———. *The Lost Cause: A New Southern History of the War of the Confederates.* New York: E. B. Treat and Co., 1866.

SECONDARY SOURCES

Anderson, Carol. *One Person, No Vote: How Voter Suppression Is Destroying Our Democracy.* New York: Bloomsbury Publishing, 2019.

———. *White Rage: The Unspoken Truth of Our Racial Divide.* New York: Bloomsbury Publishing, 2017.

Belew, Kathleen. *Bring the War Home: The White Power Movement and Paramilitary America.* Reprint ed., Cambridge, Mass.: Harvard University Press, 2019.

Blight, David W. *American Oracle: The Civil War in the Civil Rights Era.* Cambridge, Mass.: Belknap Press, 2011.

———. "'For Something beyond the Battlefield': Frederick Douglass and the Struggle for the Memory of the Civil War." *Journal of American History* 75, no. 4 (March 1989): 1156–78.

———. *Race and Reunion: The Civil War in American Memory.* Cambridge, Mass.: Belknap Press, 2001.

Brown, Thomas J. *Civil War Monuments and the Militarization of America.* Chapel Hill: University of North Carolina Press, 2019.

———. *The Public Art of Civil War Commemoration.* Boston: Bedford/ St. Martin's, 2004.

Brown, Trent, ed. *White Masculinity in the Recent South.* Baton Rouge: Louisiana State University Press, 2008.

Carney, Court. "'The Most Manly in the World': Nathan Bedford Forrest and the Cult of Southern Masculinity." In *White Masculinity in the Recent South,* edited by Trent Brown, 172–85.

Catton, Bruce. *The Coming Fury.* New York: Doubleday, 1961.

The Civil War Centennial: A Report to Congress. Washington, D.C.: Civil War Centennial Commission, 1968.

Clinton, Catherine, et al. *Confederate Statues and Memorialization.* Athens: University of Georgia Press, 2019.

Cook, Robert J. *Troubled Commemoration: The American Civil War Centennial, 1961–1965.* Baton Rouge: Louisiana State University Press, 2007.

———. "(Un)Furl That Banner: The Response of White Southerners to the Civil War Centennial of 1961–1965." *Journal of Southern History* 68, no. 4 (November 2002): 879–912.

Coski, John M. *The Confederate Battle Flag: America's Most Embattled Emblem.* Cambridge, Mass.: Belknap Press, 2006.

Cox, Karen L. *Dixie's Daughters: The United Daughters of the Confederacy and the Preservation of Confederate Culture.* Gainesville: University Press of Florida, 2003. Reprinted in 2019 with a new preface.

————. *Dreaming of Dixie: How the South Was Created in American Popular Culture.* Chapel Hill: University of North Carolina Press, 2011.

Domby, Adam H. *The False Cause: Fraud, Fabrication, and White Supremacy in Confederate Memory.* Charlottesville: University of Virginia Press, 2020.

Du Bois, W. E. B. "The Perfect Vacation." *The Crisis,* August 1931.

Eagles, Charles W. *The Price of Defiance: James Meredith and the Integration of Ole Miss.* Chapel Hill: University of North Carolina Press, 2014.

Emancipation Centennial: A Brief Anthology of the Preliminary Proclamation. Washington, D.C.: Civil War Centennial Commission, 1962.

Fields, Mamie Garvin, with Karen Fields. *Lemon Swamp and Other Places: A Carolina Memoir.* New York: The Free Press, 1983.

Forman, James. *Sammy Younge, Jr.: The First Black College Student to Die in the Black Liberation Movement.* New York: Grove Press, 1968.

Foster, Gaines M. *Ghosts of the Confederacy: Defeat, the Lost Cause, and the Emergence of the New South, 1865–1913.* New York: Oxford University Press, 1987.

Goudsouzian, Aram. *Down to the Crossroads: Civil Rights, Black Power, and the Meredith March against Fear.* New York: Farrar, Straus, and Giroux, 2014.

Green, Hilary N. "Confederate Monument Removal, 2015–2020: A Mapping Project." https://hgreen.people.ua.edu/csa-monument-mapping-project .html.

Ifill, Sherrilyn A. *On the Courthouse Lawn: Confronting the Legacy of Lynching in the Twenty-First Century.* Rev. ed. Boston: Beacon Press, 2018.

Janney, Caroline E. *Burying the Dead but Not the Past: Ladies Memorial Associations and the Lost Cause.* Chapel Hill: University of North Carolina Press, 2008.

————. *Remembering the Civil War: Reunion and the Limits of Reconciliation.* Chapel Hill: University of North Carolina Press, 2016.

Kytle, Ethan J., and Blain Roberts. *Denmark Vesey's Garden: Slavery and Memory in the Cradle of the Confederacy.* New York: New Press, 2018.

Levin, Kevin M. *Searching for Black Confederates: The Civil War's Most Persistent Myth.* Chapel Hill: University of North Carolina Press, 2019.

Levinson, Sanford. *Written in Stone: Public Monuments in Changing Societies.* Durham, N.C.: Duke University Press, Twentieth Anniversary Edition, 2018.

Lucey, Donna M. "Brother from the Richmond Planet." *Humanities* (July/ August 2010): 21–23.

Maddex, Jack P., Jr. *The Reconstruction of Edward A. Pollard: A Rebel's Conversion to Postbellum Unionism.* Chapel Hill: University of North Carolina Press, 2011.

Maxwell, Angie, and Todd Shields. *The Long Southern Strategy: How Chasing White Voters in the South Changed American Politics.* New York: Oxford University Press, 2019.

McMillen, Neil R. *The Citizens' Council: Organized Resistance to the Second Reconstruction, 1954–1964.* Champaign: University of Illinois Press, 1994.

————, ed. *Remaking Dixie: The Impact of World War II on the American South.* Jackson: University Press of Mississippi, 1997.

Meredith, James. *Three Years in Mississippi*. Jackson: University Press of Mississippi, 2019.

———. *A Mission from God: A Memoir and Challenge for America*. New York: Atria Books, 2016.

Merritt, Keri Leigh. *Masterless Men: Poor Whites and Slavery in the Antebellum South*. New York: Cambridge University Press, 2017.

Mickey, Robert. *Paths Out of Dixie: The Democratization of Authoritarian Enclaves in America's Deep South, 1944–1972*. Princeton, N.J.: Princeton University Press, 2015.

Neff, John R. *Honoring the Civil War Dead: Commemoration and the Problem of Reconciliation*. Lawrence: University Press of Kansas, 2005.

Phelps, Jess R., and Jessica Owley. "Etched in Stone: Historic Preservation Law and Confederate Monuments." *Florida Law Review* 71 (2019): 627–88.

Pratt, Robert A. *The Color of Their Skin: Education and Race in Richmond, Virginia, 1954–1989*. Charlottesville: University Press of Virginia, 1992.

Prince, K. Michael. "Neo-Confederates in the Basement: the League of the South and the Crusade against Southern Emasculation." In *White Masculinity in the Recent South*, edited by Trent Brown, 146–71.

Reddick, L. D. *Crusader without Violence: A Biography of Martin Luther King, Jr.* New York: Harper, 1959.

Richardson, Heather Cox. *How the South Won the Civil War: Oligarchy, Democracy, and the Continuing Fight for the Soul of America*. New York: Oxford University Press, 2020.

Rolph, Stephanie R. *Resisting Equality: The Citizens' Council, 1954–1989*. Baton Rouge: Louisiana State University Press, 2018.

Rose, Mrs. S. E. F. *The Ku Klux Klan or Invisible Empire*. New Orleans: L. Graham Co., 1914.

Savage, Kirk. *Standing Soldiers, Kneeling Slaves: Race, War, and Monuments in Nineteenth-Century America*. Princeton, N.J.: Princeton University Press, 1997.

Tell, Dave. *Remembering Emmett Till*. Chicago: University of Chicago Press, 2019.

Tyson, Timothy B. *The Blood of Emmett Till*. New York: Simon and Schuster, 2017.

Wahlers, Kasi E. "North Carolina's Heritage Protection Act: Cementing Confederate Monuments in North Carolina's Landscape." *North Carolina Law Review* 94, no. 6 (2016): 2176–2200.

Warrick, Alyssa D. "'Mississippi's Greatest Hour': The Mississippi Civil War Centennial and Southern Resistance." *Southern Cultures* 19, no. 3 (September 2013): 95–112.

Whites, LeeAnn. *The Civil War as a Crisis in Gender: Augusta, Georgia, 1860–1890*. Athens: University of Georgia Press, 2000.

Widener, Ralph. W., Jr. *Confederate Monuments: Enduring Symbols of the South and the War Between the States*. Washington, D.C.: Andromeda Associates, 1982.

Wilson, Charles Reagan. *Baptized in Blood: The Religion of the Lost Cause, 1865–1920*. 2nd ed. Athens: University of Georgia Press, 2009.

INDEX

Trump, Donald J., 5, 25, 153, 163–64, 172
Tubman, Harriet, 170, 172
Tuck, William M., 78
Tulane, Paul, 40
Tuskegee Institute, 99–100, 102
Tyson, James, 154

Uncle Tom's Cabin (Stowe), 16
"understanding clauses," 19–20
United Daughters of the Confederacy (UDC), 21, 55, 64, 71; children indoctrinated by, 1, 22–23, 48, 72, 74, 81; during Civil War centennial, 78; Confederate veterans and widows aided by, 1, 48; declining influence of, 171; during First World War, 54; founding of, 2; growth of, 46; headquarters of, 74–76, 170; ladies' memorial associations linked to, 49, 50; leadership of, 47; monuments promoted and funded by, 2, 4, 22, 23, 46, 48, 51–52, 67, 80, 85, 107, 110, 125, 144; public awareness of, 170; white supremacy linked to, 15
U.S. Capitol, 48
U.S. Civil War Centennial Commission, (CWCC), 78–80
Unite the Right rally (Charlottesville, 2017), 6, 25, 142, 148, 160–64
University of Alabama, 106
University of Louisville, 141–43
University of Mississippi, 84–89, 93
University of North Carolina, 105–6, 167
University of Virginia, 161

Vance, Zebulon, 117
Van Gunden, Young, and Grimm, 33
Venable, James, 107
Vesey, Denmark, 150
Vicksburg National Military Park, 80
voting rights, 5, 19, 46, 62–63, 93, 125–26, 166
Voting Rights Act (1965), 70, 91, 92, 109, 120, 147, 166

Walker, Edwin, 85–86, 87
Walker, Larry, 110–16, 118–19
Walker, Scott, 153
Wallace, George, 70–71, 106
Warrick, Alyssa, 79
Washington, Booker T., 172
Wells, Henry, 105
Wharton, A. C., Jr., 156
White League, 132
Whittington, James, 110–11, 112
Wilayto, Phil, 165
Wilder, L. Douglas, 135, 136
Williams, Hosea, 96
Williams, Mrs. Charles J., 31
Williams, Neil, 117
Williamson, Cecil, 139–40
Wilson, Charles Reagan, 29
Wilson, Hersey, 129
Wilson, Woodrow, 54
Withrow, Joe, 113
Woodward, C. Vann, 134
World's Industrial and Cotton Centennial Exposition (1884), 41
Wyndon, David, 127

Young, Andrew, *97*
Younge, Sammy, Jr., 99–103, *101, 103*